Marlowe R. Scott

Worth the Journey: The Train Ride to Glory

Copyright © 2016
Marlowe R. Scott

All Rights Reserved.
No portion of this publication may be reproduced, stored in any electronic system, or transmitted in any form or by any means (electronic, mechanical, photocopy, recording, or otherwise) without written permission from the author or publisher. Brief quotations may be used in literary reviews.

ISBN 13: 978-1945117473
ISBN 10: 1945117478
Library of Congress Control Number: 2017930024

Unless otherwise indicated, scripture references are taken from the King James Version of the Holy Bible.

For information and bulk ordering, contact:
Pearly Gates Publishing LLC
Angela R. Edwards
P.O. Box 62287
Houston, TX 77205
BestSeller@PearlyGatesPublishing.com

DEDICATION

*"I thank my God upon every
remembrance of you."*
Philippians 1:3

This book is dedicated to my special cousins: Elder Arlene Powell Holden and Marian Hubbard Wynder.

Cousin Arlene: A playmate on countless Sunday afternoons when I was young. You continually offer love, support, and prayers. You, too, have used your God-given talents for God's people through your preaching, teaching, writing, and poetry - just to mention a few of the ways you continue to bless and comfort others, especially *ME*.

Cousin Marian: A companion when taking piano lessons together. You have shared your gifts and talents in many ways: organist, church officer, dedicated missionary, and repeated responsible delegate representing your church well. Your leadership and advice are *priceless*.

Both of you are like older sisters to me. The three of us have been *BLESSED* with many delightful *"Cousin Days"* where we eat, chat, reminisce, laugh, and enjoy the memories. **THANK YOU!**

ACKNOWLEDGEMENTS

To **God** be the **GLORY** for all **HE** has done and is doing in my life.

Never-ending love and appreciation to my daughter, **Angela R. Edwards**. As CEO of Pearly Gates Publishing LLC, she has the spiritual keenness of mind, professionalism, and creativity to see that my writings are presented to the finest. Numerous others have been blessed by her allowing God to use her, and I am sure many more will be blessed through her ministry and the books her company publishes.

In my Best-Selling book, *Keeping it Real: The Straight and Narrow*, there were some written reviews given by readers. One was inadvertently left out, and it follows. The review is from Brother Walter Brown, Past President of the Senior Choir and Past President of QUEST Outreach Ministry of Tabernacle Baptist Church, Burlington, New Jersey. His review states: "*This book offers an in-depth look at Believing Without Seeing with numerous helpful references. Although it was brief, it was well-written and easily understood. This book is alive and active and compels the reader's focus on the true meaning of faith, such as believing in God, trusting in God, abiding in Him, etc.*" Thank you, Brother Brown!

Worth the Journey: The Train Ride to Glory

INTRODUCTION

With this three-in-one collection of my award-winning books, I believe the words and messages have come full circle. My continued prayer and desire is that others come to accept, know, and love Jesus Christ as I do and experience the Christian journey to its *fullest*!

As we grow and personally know the comfort of being a child of the King of Kings and Lord of Lords, we know the certainty of experiencing the love, joy, and peace that is found no other way. There are pages to journal and make notes, as well as thought-provoking questions to answer contained herein.

Note that the train on the cover has the numbers **"119"**. This made me think of the Psalmist, King David - the man after God's own heart. The Psalm contains the 22 letters of the Hebrew alphabet, and each verse division has eight lines. It is a spiritual poetic guideline for obeying God's laws and walking the spiritual pathway. It begins with those clearly-understood words, *"Blessed are the undefiled in the way, who walk in the law of the Lord"*.

Marlowe R. Scott

Additionally, Psalm 119:105 is the theme verse for the Pioneer Club at my church, Tabernacle Baptist Church in Burlington, New Jersey. Indeed, God's Word is a **"Lamp"** and **"Light"** for us.

Recently, a poem which I had written for the 80th church anniversary for Tabernacle Baptist Church was found. May it enlighten and strengthen you.

Worth the Journey: The Train Ride to Glory

KINSHIP BENEFITS
Marlowe Scott © 2013

While it may be important to feel we have
achieved success in this earthly life,
The greatest success is having kinship with
Jesus and promised Eternal Life.

Kinship for Christians means
we have a blood connection
Which Jesus sacrificially shed
during his crucifixion.

We are adopted son and daughters
of the Most High
And receive those benefits that this
earth's money cannot buy.

David's beautiful Psalm 103:2,
makes it very clear:
We must not forget all God's benefits
while we dwell here.

This makes us assured
that when problems do come,
We can turn to Christ Jesus -
our Savior and Almighty One.

Marlowe R. Scott

You will experience protection and blessings
others need to come to know.
For those outside of the Ark of Safety, we know
when life ends where they will go.

If that is not enough, we further find in
Philippians 4:7 confirmation
That our hearts and minds are kept safe
through Christ Jesus in any situation.

Ephesians 6:10-18 teaches us
how to spiritually dress
To combat Satan when he starts up his mess.

Before ascending to His Father in Heaven,
Jesus gave us promised peace
in John 14:27.

We **ARE** the children of the
One and Only True God;
Why men still resist Him seems really odd.

An open invitation is offered for anyone
to join in as God's adopted child;
His Word is true and unchanging -
be assured the choice is worthwhile.

Worth the Journey: The Train Ride to Glory

TABLE OF CONTENTS

DEDICATION V

ACKNOWLEDGEMENTS VI

INTRODUCTION VII

BOOK - SPIRITUAL GROWTH: FROM MILK TO STRONG MEAT

CHAPTER ONE: BABE IN CHRIST YEARS 8

CHAPTER TWO: YOUTH IN CHRIST YEARS 14

CHAPTER THREE: ADULT IN CHRIST YEARS 22

CHAPTER FOUR: SENIOR IN CHRIST YEARS 31

BOOK - BELIEVING WITHOUT SEEING: THE POWER OF FAITH

OLD TESTAMENT FAITH HEROES 58

FRUIT OF THE SPIRIT 67

JESUS' ASCENSION AND GIFTS 81

ADDENDUM: "THE ABUSIVE AND UNRULY TONGUE" 85

BOOK - KEEPING IT REAL: THE STRAIGHT AND NARROW

A SPECIAL NOTE FROM PRESIDENT OBAMA & FAMILY 112

CHAPTER ONE: KEEPING IT REAL 124

CHAPTER TWO: THE DEVIL GOES TO CHURCH 129

Marlowe R. Scott

CHAPTER THREE: MOUNTAIN CLIMBING 141

CHAPTER FOUR: HIGH PLACES 150

CHAPTER FIVE: PRESSING UPWARD 159

CHAPTER SIX: THE EMPTY CROSS 166

BENEDICTION 171

CONCLUSION.. 172

TESTIMONIES AND INSIGHTS... 173

AMAZON BEST-SELLING BOOKS WRITTEN BY MARLOWE R. SCOTT 179

ABOUT THE AUTHOR 182

Worth the Journey: The Train Ride to Glory

Marlowe R. Scott

Worth the Journey: The Train Ride to Glory

DEDICATION

This book is dedicated to the
memories of my parents,
Carl Edward
and
Helena Rachel (Winrow) Harris,
and to my special brother,
Harry Elmer Harris,
who spent many quality hours
of his life with me.

ACKNOWLEDGEMENTS

First, giving thanks to **God** for salvation through His Son, Jesus Christ, as well as for my spiritual gifts and talents.

For my husband, **Andrew Scott**, I thank you for your patience in allowing me time and opportunity to pursue my gifts.

Angela's Accurate Administrative Services: Thank you for your professional suggestions and support.

To **Pearly Gates Publishing LLC**: I am appreciative of your promptness, availability, and comprehension of my vision and needs.

AUTHOR'S PRAYER FOR THE READER

Heavenly Father, may everyone reading this book be encouraged to grow in their personal relationship with our Lord and Savior, Jesus Christ. For those who have not accepted Christ as their personal Savior, I pray a seed be planted so they, too, will seek to know Him. During troubled times, my prayer is that the reader learns Jesus is always there and that God will not allow His children to experience more than they can bear. Finally, I pray that each one is led to and attending a Bible preaching *and* teaching church where sound, biblical doctrine is taught.

All these things I ask in the Precious Name of Your Son, Jesus Christ.
AMEN.

Worth the Journey: The Train Ride to Glory

INTRODUCTION

"As newborn babies, desire the sincere milk of the word, that ye may grow thereby: If so be you have tasted that the Lord is gracious." 1 Peter 2:2-3

Inspiration for this writing comes from the realization that my life has changed, my spiritual life has been enriched, and I am continually learning the value of Jesus Christ, salvation, and the unmerited love, protection, and mercy I have from being a Born-Again Christian.

The purpose and ultimate outcome of these shared experiences are three-fold:

1. To share how spiritual growth affords the opportunity to teach and witness to others;
2. To encourage others to become believers in Jesus Christ and join in Christian service while on this earthly journey; and
3. To emphasize that the Christian walk is a journey that is not always smooth, but worth every moment!

A hymn written by M. E. Abbey in 1933 entitled "Life's Railway to Heaven" was a favorite of my father and has great meaning for me. The song clearly illustrates there are curves, tunnels, trials, and obstructions in life – but ultimate victory is achieved through the love, grace, and mercy of Jesus Christ. I ask you to come and ride this journey with me.

(*NOTE: Verses of the hymn are quoted at the beginning of each stage of my Christian walk and life's story.*)

Worth the Journey: The Train Ride to Glory

SPIRITUAL GROWTH

From Milk to Strong Meat

"For every one that useth milk is unskillful in the word of righteousness; for he is a babe. But strong meat belongeth to them that are of full age, even those who by reason of use have their senses exercised to discern both good and evil."
Hebrews 5:13-14

CHAPTER 1
Babe in Christ Years

"Train up a child in the way he should go: and when he is old, he will not depart from it." Proverbs 22:6

VERSE 1: LIFE IS LIKE A MOUNTAIN RAILROAD

"Life is like a mountain railroad, with an engineer that's brave; We must make the run successful, from the cradle to the grave; Watch the curves, the fills, the tunnels; never falter, never quail; Keep your hand upon the throttle, and your eye upon the rail."

Worth the Journey: The Train Ride to Glory

As a child reared in a Christian home and on the cradle-roll of my home church, John Wesley United Methodist Church, Bridgeton, NJ, I can truly say my journey has been from the cradle to (one day) the grave.

My earliest memories as a young child include learning prayers that were to be recited before meals and at bedtime. I was also read Bible stories and learned songs such as *Jesus Loves Me* and *Jesus Wants Me for a Sunbeam*. Because my family attended church regularly, I began Sunday school in the Nursery Class and learned several children's songs from the Methodist hymnal. Once I began to speak clearly, I participated yearly in the Easter and Christmas programs by both singing and reciting poems.

As a pre-teen, I joined a children's organization called "The Loyal Temperance Legion" – an after-school program that taught discipline, self-control, and salvation. A theme we learned during the meetings was something which remains with me today: "Dare to be a Daniel, Dare to Stand Alone, Dare to Make a Promise True, Dare to Make it Known". It was through the program combined with learning about Jesus from church that I accepted Jesus as my personal Savior at the age of nine.

I must mention that during those formative years, I spent a lot of time with my brother, Harry, who was mentally-challenged. On several occasions, we would "play church", sing songs, and take turns praying by kneeling at the foot of the stairs leading upstairs.

Going to church and worshipping remained a part of Harry's life until he could no longer attend. He believed in prayer and would pray before meals and even for someone who was ill. Harry was loving, giving, and kind.

The following poem was inspired in the 1990s and shares an important message about my friend, Jesus.

Worth the Journey: The Train Ride to Glory

JESUS, MY FRIEND JESUS
Marlowe R. Scott © 1995

What a friend we have in Jesus;
He all our sins and grief will bear.
Our friend, Jesus, came and left Someone special
When He ascended to His Father in the air!

The Comforter, the Holy Spirit,
Surrounds each of us every day and everywhere;
Because our Beloved Counselor and Friend, Jesus,
Left the Holy Spirit here – when He joined His Father in the air!

But wait – Do you really know my friend, Jesus?
Does He all your burdens bear?
Are you really ready to meet and greet Him
When He descends again – coming down through the air?

If not, then I invite you today to receive Him
And enjoy the friendly, bountiful love I share
With our Lord and Savior, Jesus Christ,
Who reigns in Heaven with God – up there in the air!

Come quickly! Praise and celebrate with me!
A Friend who loves unconditionally, without compare;
His name is Emanuel – Wonderful Jesus, be ye ready to meet Him
When He comes again from Glory – shouting through the air!

Marlowe R. Scott

REFLECTIONS

Worth the Journey: The Train Ride to Glory

CHAPTER 2
Youth in Christ Years

"Remember now thy Creator in the days of thy youth, while the evil days come not, nor the years draw nigh, when thou shalt say, I have no pleasure in them;"
Ecclesiastes 12:2

VERSE 2: LIFE IS LIKE A MOUNTAIN RAILROAD
"You will roll up grades of trial; you will cross the bridge of strife; See that Christ is your Conductor on this lightning train of life; Always mindful of obstruction, do your duty, never fail; Keep your hands upon the throttle, and your eye upon the rail."

Worth the Journey: The Train Ride to Glory

During the time when religion was allowed in public schools, the graduating class of 1962 from Bridgeton High School had a voice choir which I was part of as the lead speaker. The scripture recited for the occasion was the familiar (for some) Ecclesiastes 3:1-8.

1To everything there is a season, and a time to every purpose under the heaven:
2 A time to be born, and a time to die; a time to plant, and a time to pluck up that which is planted;
3 A time to kill, and a time to heal; a time to break down, and a time to build up;
4 A time to weep, and a time to laugh; a time to mourn, and a time to dance;
5 A time to cast away stones, and a time to gather stones together; a time to embrace, and a time to refrain from embracing;
6 A time to get, and a time to lose; a time to keep, and a time to cast away;
7 A time to rend, and a time to sew; a time to keep silence, and a time to speak;
8 A time to love, and a time to hate; a time of war, and a time of peace.

Indeed, as I have matured, I really know that there is a season and purpose for everything under the heavens. My years of youth also included attending educational Christian conferences, Methodist Youth Fellowship, and singing in the youth choir.

Marlowe R. Scott

Growing up in John Wesley United Methodist Church has many, many memories worth sharing – far too many to detail here. A few of my personal favorites are attached to the old-fashioned church picnics in the park with my mother's fried chicken and best potato salad EVER! In addition, on most Sundays after church, we would visit cousins, older uncles and aunts, and have great times building countless memories (I can't forget to mention the good food).

In the "good, old days" (as my oldest son, Carl, would say), we had only one pair of church shoes and a couple sets of "Sunday's best" clothes. Easter and Christmas were special because something new would be added to the wardrobe.

Sidebar: Speaking of Christmas, our Sunday school gave us an apple, orange, and candy cane after our Sunday school exercises for the Christmas program. We appreciated the simplicity of the gifts.

My family lived in the farming and canning factory area of South Jersey. For Thanksgiving, we had an annual "Harvest Home" at church where baskets of vegetables, fruits, and the ladies' home-canned goods would be placed around the altar and blessed before distribution to the members and other needy families.

Worth the Journey: The Train Ride to Glory

I fondly recall the church members always encouraging the other children and me with smiles and applause for our songs and recitations. When I began taking piano lessons at the age of nine, they even clapped when I played my one-handed melodies. Even at that young age, my goal was to learn how to play hymns and Christian songs – with *both* hands!

Another vivid memory was my first opportunity to be a youth delegate for a conference at Haverford College in Pennsylvania. It was there, during one of the sessions, that I was able to learn more about worldly "knowledge" and Christian "belief".

There is a plethora of knowledge that can be learned through education and experience; however, as a Christian, you must personally have faith and believe in your very soul that Jesus Christ is the Savior. Only through repentance and believing in Him will you reach eternity in Heaven when death comes. We must continually study the Holy Bible and pray while seeking the truth and growing spiritually.

My mother was a well-known Christian soprano in the local churches. She taught me many songs and let me accompany her to choir rehearsals and other events. The following poem I penned recalls many fond memories of my mother.

SONGS IN THE NIGHT
Marlowe R. Scott © 2014

God speaks to me in many pleasant ways
Throughout each day and night;
Through the whispering trees and
flowering fields,
Babbling brooks and lovely,
chirping birds in flight.

Often in the quiet stillness of the night,
My Heavenly Father also speaks from above
With beautiful words, melodies, and song
That inspire and confirm His unending love.

Songs that my mother once sang
Or those I learned as a child;
All of those precious renderings
Have comforted me through many a trial.

The drums, tambourine, flute and pipe;
The harp, timbrel, trumpet, and lyre –
Many musical instruments are in
God's Holy Word,
All making joyful noise to set my soul on fire!

Worth the Journey: The Train Ride to Glory

"Songs in the Night" continued…

The Bible's Old Testament as well as the New
Tell of melodies and songs of praise,
as well as blessings
That many such as Moses, Isaiah,
and David offered
For Strength and protection from
Lucifer's attempted messings.

Even one of troubled Job's young friends, Elihu,
Acknowledged that God giveth
songs in the night (Job 35:10);
In the end, Job's blessings increased
two-fold (Job 42:10);
Who wouldn't trust and serve a God with that
power and might!

So, just listen my sisters and brothers,
As God speaks to you in His various ways;
Remember – His messages are clear,
tried, and true;
Seek to hear, oh hear Him, each and every day.

Marlowe R. Scott
REFLECTIONS

Worth the Journey: The Train Ride to Glory

CHAPTER 3
Adult in Christ Years

"The Lord is my strength and my shield; my heart trusted in Him, and I am helped: therefore my heart greatly rejoiceth; and with my song will I praise Him." Psalm 28:7

VERSE 3: LIFE IS LIKE A MOUNTAIN RAILROAD

"You will often find obstructions; look for storms of wind and rain; On a fill, or curve, or trestle, they will almost ditch your train; Put your trust alone in Jesus; never falter, never fail; Keep your hands upon the throttle, and your eye upon the rail."

Worth the Journey: The Train Ride to Glory

Broken relationships, children to raise, and the loss of my parents. My adult years were possibly my humanly roughest period.

By growing and understanding how Jesus fights my battles when I allow Him to, I definitely know everything works out for the best.

I recall a December when there were joint community choir rehearsals preparing for New Year's Eve services. There was much conversation about the news announcing that Fort Dix, New Jersey was again on the Base Closure List. I sat quietly – waiting for all the talk to cease and choir rehearsal to begin. Finally, someone looked at me and said, "You work at Fort Dix. What are you going to do?" My response was simply, "I believe God will take care of my family and me – just as He always has in the past." Needless to say, the excessive talking stopped and we began rehearsing. Not only was I taken care of, but I also received a promotion early the next year!

Another invaluable lesson I learned was to pray for those who may unjustly persecute you (Matthew 5:44). This occurred when I openly told a military supervisor that I was praying for him after he refused to understand my responsibilities outside of work. The result was that I received a promotion out of that office. Looking back, I appreciate the many doors only God could open when they were shut by man. Personal experiences with others, negative work situations, and other types of discrimination have always proven that God will offer a way out. In addition, there was the irrefutable proof that the next step was higher and better than I had ever anticipated.

There are many instances where God has taken care of me and provided protection. On one occasion while driving home during my 40-mile one-way trip from work, I was slowing to a stop at a red light on a busy highway. I looked in my rearview mirror and saw one of those older, large, and well-built cars barreling down the road behind me. Behind the wheel was an elderly gentleman – a PhD scientist – nodding off at the wheel. I only had time to say out loud, "**JESUS!**" – and his car stopped.

Worth the Journey: The Train Ride to Glory

Another important area of my spiritual walk was discovering and using the Spiritual Gifts God gives to each believer. One of mine is the Spiritual Gift of Faith. In 1 Corinthians 12:9, it says, "To another faith by the same Spirit..." Faith is an assurance and belief. The author of Hebrews 11:1 wrote, "Now faith is the substance of things hoped for, the evidence of things not seen." The gift of Faith involves a prompting from God to trust Him for the supernatural and to continue even when there are difficult circumstances.

The gift of Faith was demonstrated at a time when I was raising my children alone. I knew God would keep His promise to never forsake me and to continually provide shelter and food for us. On one occasion, I exercised my Faith Spiritual Gift, even though I did not fully understand at the time all that God had given me in that area. I put my very last bit of money in a church sacrificial offering, and that week, I received unexpected food and provisions to sustain my family!

Marlowe R. Scott

On another occasion, after giving an aunt a hairdryer she badly needed, I stopped on the way home at a yard sale where two lovely senior citizens were combining households and downsizing. I had my children with me and spent time in casual conversation with the couple. The next day, which was Sunday, somehow the couple found my home and gave me plush towels and linens – items I would have never been able to afford at the time.

In an effort to witness and spread the Word through literature, I also sold Christian books through a party plan. As a part of each demonstration (and to set the appropriate tone for the presentation), I sang the familiar words of "If I Can Help Somebody", which was my sincerest desire then and now. My daughter, Angela, accompanied me to parties and book fairs where the seed was planted to enjoy reading quality literature while learning administrative skills. Due to these experiences, she is now providing a wide variety of services through her virtual home-based business, Angela's Accurate Administrative Services. Her newest book-publishing venture (with the distinctive name Pearly Gates Publishing, LLC) has been instrumental in seeing this publication come to fruition.

Worth the Journey: The Train Ride to Glory

In each church that I was a member of, I became involved in many ministries: Sunday School Teacher, Choir and Willing Workers President, Secretary, and other areas of Christian Education. As a member of the African American Episcopal Church, I held the office of the Atlantic City District Lay President for 31 churches in southern New Jersey for four years.

Because my initial Christian training was received in the Methodist church, I was christened as an infant. Upon joining the Baptist denomination, I had to be water baptized in a pool. That glorious occasion was on December 15, 1993 in Florence, New Jersey!

After hearing a series of sermons about Jesus, The True Vine, yet another poem was inspired stressing the need for Christians to be connected to the spiritual power source: Jesus.

HIGHER SPIRITUAL HEIGHTS
Marlowe R. Scott © 2013

The man of God came preaching and teaching
About Jesus, the Savior and True Vine;
It is the message of being connected
To the Messiah, who came to save all mankind!

The congregation was excited by the Word
And felt the Holy Spirit's fire;
God used the preacher as a messenger
To edify and lift Jesus higher!

The preacher's sermon about the
Day of Pentecost
Gave thirsty souls high spiritual blessings
and insight;
The congregation rejoiced and praised God
For the valuable lesson on growing in this
spiritual fight!

As the man of God continues to lead,
Everything – yes everything – will be alright;
For thirsting souls to grow and be blessed
Until reaching God's promised
Heavenly Heights!

Worth the Journey: The Train Ride to Glory

REFLECTIONS

Marlowe R. Scott

CHAPTER 4
Senior in Christ Years

"Now that I speak in respect of want; for I have learned, in whatsoever state I am, therewith to be content."
Philippians 4:13

VERSE 4 and REFRAIN: LIFE IS LIKE A MOUNTAIN RAILROAD

"As you roll across the trestle, spanning Jordan's swelling tide; You behold the Union Depot into which your train will glide; There you'll meet the Superintendent, God the Father, God the Son; With the hearty, joyous plaudit,
"Weary pilgrim, welcome home!""

(Refrain)
"Blessed Savior, Thou wilt guide us,
Till we reach that blissful shore;
Where the angels wait to join us
In Thy praise forevermore."

I can definitely say this season of my life is truly the "Golden Years".

After lifelong church attendance and conversion for 60+ years, one might think there is not much more for me to learn about the need for Christian growth. **WRONG!**

The reasons are many, but the focus here is on the Bible study classes in church on Wednesday nights. They have made a great impact on my current spiritual growth. In particular, there were two classes that heightened my awareness: Spiritual Warfare and Apologetics.

Spiritual Warfare was very spiritually-enlightening because I learned more about those forces written in Ephesians 6:10-18 that speak of spiritual warfare and how we must spiritually "dress" ourselves each day.

[10] *Finally, my brethren, be strong in the Lord, and in the power of his might.*

[11] *Put on the whole armour of God, that ye may be able to stand against the wiles of the devil.*

[12] *For we wrestle not against flesh and blood, but against principalities, against powers, against the rulers of the darkness of this world, against spiritual wickedness in high places.*

Worth the Journey: The Train Ride to Glory

¹³ Wherefore take unto you the whole armour of God, that ye may be able to withstand in the evil day, and having done all, to stand.

¹⁴ Stand therefore, having your loins girt about with truth, and having on the breastplate of righteousness;

¹⁵ And your feet shod with the preparation of the gospel of peace;

¹⁶ Above all, taking the shield of faith, wherewith ye shall be able to quench all the fiery darts of the wicked.

¹⁷ And take the helmet of salvation, and the sword of the Spirit, which is the word of God:

¹⁸ Praying always with all prayer and supplication in the Spirit, and watching thereunto with all perseverance and supplication for all saints;

Having experienced so much on my journey, I now better understand how to apply the scriptures, pray for discernment, and combat Satan's deceptions and lies.

The Spiritual Warfare course excited me to the point that I wrote an article for the church newsletter. Following are excerpts from the article for edification and further information:

"Attending the Spiritual Warfare classes created another "spurt" in my spiritual growth. The in-depth study of Spiritual Warfare took time to teach specific areas of how to attack and apply our spiritual weapons to resist and conquer Satan's negative influence on ourselves, family, and friends. Just realizing the need to learn about this daily warfare battle is more than a spiritual blessing; it is eye-opening and causes some personal soul-searching."

"Our book of study is primarily from the Holy Bible. We also used a book entitled *Pigs in the Parlor* by Frank and Ida Mae Hammond. The title may sound strange, but consider the following question: If you had dirty, smelly pigs ruining your parlor by destroying your home, spreading disease and filth, what would you do? The obvious answer is GET RID OF THEM and do it QUICKLY! Likewise, we, as Christians, are directed to get rid of Satan's negative and destroying spiritual interferences in our walk with our Lord and Savior, Jesus Christ – and to do it quickly, the same as we would do to pigs in our homes!"

Worth the Journey: The Train Ride to Glory

The Apologetics class taught ways to better relate and witness to others who do not believe as we do. That is accomplished by asking questions and developing a dialog with them. We are encouraged to be Ambassadors for Christ. Although not always easy, we are cautioned in God's Word when it says, "Let your speech be always with grace, seasoned with salt, that ye may know how ye ought to answer every man" (Colossians 4:6). While that process many not work in all situations, we are taught that some plant, some water, but only God can give the increase (1 Corinthians 3:6).

A brief summary of the aforementioned principles is this: We are to be alert for opportunities to represent Christ. We are not to be argumentative about our beliefs. We are to always be respectful of others' views and adaptable to each individual person. Additionally, do not use Christian "lingo". Keep the biblical truths plain. Be very careful in sharing the facts. The Ambassador will act with kindness, grace, and good manners – and will NOT DISHONOR CHRIST by their conduct.

As stated in a previous chapter, I love music and enjoy praising through song. When my children were young, we used to sing together at home while I played the piano. Even today, the music still comes forth through them. My "Christmas Baby", James Daryl (yes, he was born Christmas morning), is pursuing a musical degree while composing music and playing guitar.

In today's church setting, my spirit sometimes aches to hear and sing the hymns most Christian churches have in their hymn/worship books, but no longer use. To share the words of Rev. Dr. Richard W. Jones who transcended to Heaven in June 2010, "Hymns are songs 'with meat on them'." Those who are spiritually-mature recognize the depth and spirituality connected to hymns. They:

- Confirm our faith through song;
- Offer comfort and security in times of trials;
- Share God's unending love and care;
- Offer salvation to the unsaved; and
- Are forms of testimony and witness to others.

Worth the Journey: The Train Ride to Glory

Following is the last inspirational poem that came to me while thinking about what to submit to the church newsletter published by the Sheepfold Ministry. The poem tells a story of what is in store for those both inside and outside the spiritual sheepfold. It invites those outside to come in for safety and guaranteed eternal life when accepting the invitation.

Marlowe R. Scott

THE SHEEPFOLD
Marlowe R. Scott © 2015

Being a part of the Lord's Sheepfold
Is a very blessed thing
Because our Redeemer, Jesus,
Is the Keeper, Savior, and King!

When we are lost, Jesus finds us.
He picks us up and carries us back.
With Him as Protector and Leader,
No good thing shall we lack.

He is tender, gentle, and kind.
He loves us and calls each by name.
Surely, Jesus knows the pastures we need
To maintain our naïve and earthly frames.

We can sleep peacefully at night
Under the Shepherd's watchful eye.
The dawning of each new day
Guarantees that He is still nearby.

Do not be caught outside the Sheepfold;
There are dangers and death out there!
Come and stay safely inside with us
Until we transcend to Eternity in the air!

Worth the Journey: The Train Ride to Glory

REFLECTIONS

Marlowe R. Scott

CONCLUSION

I must confess that life has not been a "bed of roses" for me. Surely, there were disappointments, hurts, tears, heartaches, and many sleepless nights. However, I realize that each instance grew me stronger and wiser – in God's time. I believe that God is not through with me yet!

It is difficult to summarize the truths I have learned during my journey. As a short list, I would like to offer and share the following:

- The child's song, *Jesus Loves Me*, has been a stabilizing truth and comfort to me for over 70 years.
- I must know and be able to discern the Holy Scriptures for myself with prayer, study, and the Holy Spirit (Comforter).
- Speaking up and showing/sharing God's love can reap unmerited favor.
- It is truly better to give than receive.
- God takes care of those who despitefully or otherwise attempt to use, abuse, or mislead His children. Clearly stated, God fights my battles when I allow Him and He offers a way out of troubles and dangers.

It saddens me to add that not every preacher, leader, and member of a church professing Jesus Christ is a Christian. Found in Matthew 7:15 are these words spoken by Jesus Christ: "Beware of false prophets, which come to you in sheep's clothing, but inwardly they are ravening wolves."

My steps may be slower these days, but my soul is stronger. My spiritual life has deepened by continually reading and studying the Holy Bible and attending various Christian Education classes, as well as exercising and expressing my faith.

As the last verse of the hymn *Life's Railway to Heaven* states, one day I look forward to crossing Jordan's swelling tide. There, my soul will be welcomed by God the Father and God the Son with those precious words, **"Weary Pilgrim, Welcome Home!"**

Worth the Journey: The Train Ride to Glory

Ephesians 3:20-21

[20] Now unto him that is able to do exceeding abundantly above all that we ask or think, according to the power that worketh in us,

[21] Unto him be glory in the church by Christ Jesus throughout all ages, world without end. ***AMEN.***

Marlowe R. Scott

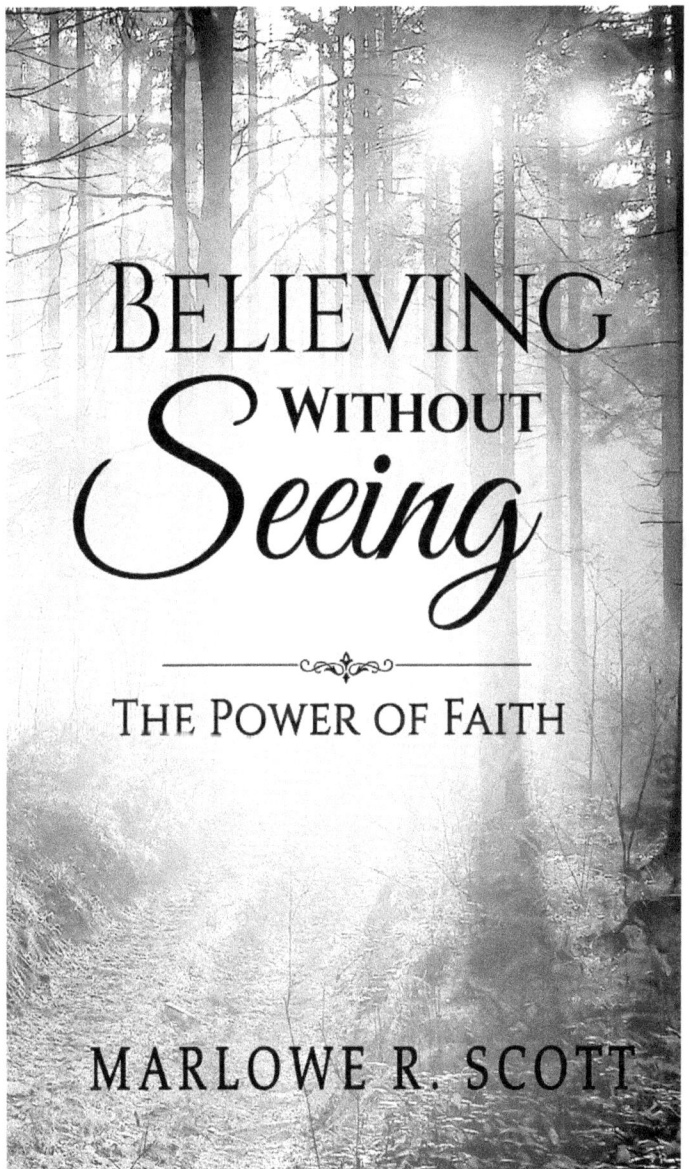

Dedication

To my family members, pastors, ministers of the Gospel of Jesus Christ, and Christian Education teachers who have sown spiritual seeds in my life, demonstrated love, and influenced my Christian Walk with Jesus Christ.

Acknowledgements

First and foremost, I thank God for His continued divine guidance, truths, and Holy Scriptures which have brought me through many mountains and valleys on this earthly journey. Because of our Heavenly Father, Jesus Christ, and the Holy Spirit, those journeys have always worked out for my best.

Secondly, to my daughter, Angela Edwards (CEO of *Pearly Gates Publishing LLC*) for love, patience, continued support, availability, and advice while bringing my second literary endeavor to fruition.

Introduction

First, let it be clear that I do not profess to be a Theologian nor Bible Scholar. I do, however, love reading and studying the Holy Bible. Through such studies, I have discovered the Spiritual Gifts that **all** Born-Again Christians have and how those gifts enrich the Body of Christ in the church when properly incorporated into the worship and teaching experiences.

As it is with many Christians, I have been blessed with more than one Spiritual Gift; however, the more prevalent one for *me* has been the Gift of **Faith**. This book will share scriptures and illustrations about Faith, as well as touch on the other Spiritual Gifts.

Mankind has found numerous ways to evade the beliefs, love, forgiveness, and salvation found truly in **FAITH IN THE ONLY TRUE GOD, HIS SON JESUS THE CHRIST, AND THE HOLY SPIRIT**. A simple childlike faith is what the Holy Scriptures tell us about in many Books from the Old Testament to the New Testament.

Worth the Journey: The Train Ride to Glory

Faith means different things to many people. It is sometimes only used when something can be seen or touched; hence the adage, "Seeing is believing". This brings to mind the times I have discussed or asked about a person's faith and I am given the name of a denomination such as Methodist, Baptist, Catholic, or the evasive, "My mother took me to church, but I personally do not go much." Others are bold enough to say they have faith only in themselves! Often in newscasts, I've heard many different members of religions classified as "The Faithful". Maybe that is *politically correct* (so to speak), but some of those religions are not always part of the faithful followers of **God** and our Lord and Savior, **Jesus Christ.**

Some of the definitions of faith found in the concordance and dictionary include: confidence, trust, credit, assurance, credence, certainty, reliance, sureness, conviction, and dependence. Steadfast means to be stable and staunch. To be faithful is to be trusting, trustworthy, unwavering, and loyal.

There are aids available to discover your personal Spiritual Gifts. While I **DO NOT** endorse any particular site that administers the Spiritual Gift Inventory, there are suggestions referenced at the end of this book. Also, I personally have found that taking the evaluation at intervals of three to five years reflects my spiritual growth and that other gifts have become more prevalent during that time; however, they remain in the same area of *service* to the church body.

As shared in my first book, *Spiritual Growth: From Milk to Strong Meat*, I love the messages found in hymns. Following is portion of a hymn by Petrus Herbert entitled *Faith is a Living Power from Heaven*:

> *"Faith finds in Christ whate'er we need*
>
> *To save or strengthen us indeed,*
>
> *Receives the grace He sends us down,*
>
> *And makes us share His cross and crown."*

Worth the Journey: The Train Ride to Glory

At the end of this publication, there is what I consider an important Addendum addressing the subject of abuse. Once again, Angela Edwards of Pearly Gates Publishing LLC is addressing the issue with a collection of those who have been abused and they share how they overcame. Included in the Addendum is an inspirational poem God gave me on July 16, 2015 - my 71st birthday!

Prayer for the Reader

Dear Jesus,

In Your Name, I offer prayer for each person who reads the words of this book. I pray their faith be strengthened and deepened, and that their Spiritual Gifts are used to glorify your kingdom here on earth. May their gifts be used in the church body without human pride or other characteristics that may interfere with their edification to the Body of Christ. Amen.

~ Marlowe R. Scott ~

Worth the Journey: The Train Ride to Glory

Theme Text

"But the fruit of the Spirit is love, joy, peace, longsuffering, gentleness, goodness, faith, meekness, temperance: against such there is no law."

Galatians 5:22-23

GROWING IN FAITH
Marlowe R. Scott © 2015

Our Spiritual Gift of Faith,
like the small mustard seed,
Is planted by God and must grow
Into a deep-rooted belief
that our Father nurtures
As the sun, winds, and storms of life
come and go.

While our fruitful day may not readily come,
God continues the sunshine and rains
And counts each budding leaf one by one.

You see: He knows the end before we do
Because all of His promises are definitely true;
and,
We must have faith to see the growing-period
through.

When we begin to mature and bear the
fruit as we should,
We will see the positive outcome of
those times we waited
And realize that our God surely has been
more than good!

Worth the Journey: The Train Ride to Glory

Goals for
Believing Without Seeing: The Power of Faith

- Provide information to foster a clearer and deeper understanding of the nine Fruit of the Spirit and Spiritual Gifts.
- Explore the Spirit of Faith given to **EACH** Born-Again Christian.
- Share biblical examples and situations where faith was exhibited.
- Ignite interest in the reader to discover their *PERSONAL* Spiritual Gift(s).

As humans, we often attribute faithfulness to many *people* and *things*. This includes a faithful mate, friend, and those in the church setting. Nature has many other examples of faithful elements, to include: our pets, the amazing "Old Faithful Geyser", the sun, moon, and perennial plants which return each year - to mention a few. Others are objects we use, such as our vehicles, machines, and equipment. *It must be noted here that without God's creation and man, we would not have **ANY** of these things.*

EXAMPLES MANKIND MAY IDENTIFY AS "FAITHFUL"- but may ultimately fail

- Vehicles – brakes may fail; tires wear out and blow out; auto-lock entry fails.
- Pets – may turn on owner/handler when they are injured and you try to help them; may have food or item in their mouth that they should not have and they growl at and/or bite you.
- Mate has an affair or divorce occurs.
- Friends use you for their benefit (i.e. money and other needs), but are not there when you have problems or need support.
- Former prolific fruit-bearing tree fails due to weather-related elements (i.e. too much heat/rain), worms, disease, or improper pollination.

FACT:

Faithful things on earth wear out, die, and eventually have an ending.

Worth the Journey: The Train Ride to Glory

Christians are taught that Hebrews 11 is the "Faith Chapter" or the "Heroes of Faith Chapter" because of the many prophets, individuals, and early believers listed. It lists the problems they faced, yet they remained steadfast and unmovable in their faith.

Many Christians can readily quote Hebrews 11:1, "Now faith is the substance of things hoped for, the evidence of things not seen." *I sincerely wonder sometimes how much this is **truly** believed or displayed.*

OLD TESTAMENT FAITH HEROES

For those who have been in church – even if only for a short time – you have probably heard the story of Job's trials, tribulations, and great losses. He never gave up his faith in his God! Should you *not* have heard his story, I encourage you to read the Book of Job and see that in the end, God **blessed** Job many times over from what he had previously.

There are, however, others in biblical history I feel are worth mentioning. The first is Caleb. He was one of the 12 men Moses appointed to go spy the land of Canaan (the land God had promised to His people after their 40 years of wandering in the wilderness after leaving Egyptian captivity). It is important to note that Caleb was from the Tribe of Judah – Jesus Christ's ancestral heritage!

Worth the Journey: The Train Ride to Glory

When the 12 chosen men reached Canaan, they found a land flowing with milk and honey as God had promised; however, there were some stumbling stones in their way from the human point of view. The land had fortified cities and giants. When they reported back to Moses, only Caleb spoke out (as noted in Numbers 13:30-31): "And Caleb stilled the people before Moses, and said, "Let us go up at once, and possess it; for we are well able to overcome it." But the men that went up with him said, "We be not able to go up against the people; for they are stronger than we.""

Not only did Caleb stand up against the majority, he displayed the **faith** and confidence that God's promises could come to fruition for the Israelites.

How many times in our lives (me included) have we **not** gone forward because of giants and other stumbling blocks in our path?

FAITH POWER POINT – *Faith KNOWS that God always keeps His promises no matter what obstacles come your way.*

There are women in the Bible who also displayed faith in their spiritual journeys. One such woman was Hannah, the mother of Samuel. Hannah was married to Elkanah and was unable to bear a child. Her husband also had another wife who taunted Hannah because she had children and Hannah did not. This, of course, hurt Hannah.

Hannah loved the Lord and went to pray to Him in Shiloh. She asked for a child and promised that if she conceived, she would dedicate the child to the Lord (see 1 Samuel 1:11). When Eli the Priest saw her praying without speaking out loud, he thought she was drunk. After telling Eli she was praying and pouring her heart out to God, Eli told her to go in peace and added a blessing that God would grant what she had asked for (see 1 Samuel 1:17).

Hannah **did** conceive and a son, Samuel, was born. As promised to God, she took the child back to Eli to be trained. There is a *beautiful* prayer of Hannah's recorded in 1 Samuel 2:1-10. For her obedience and faithfulness, Hannah was later blessed with **three** sons and **two** daughters (see 1 Samuel 2:21).

Worth the Journey: The Train Ride to Glory

FAITH POWER POINT - *Praying to God in **faith** (according to God's will) **and** keeping the promise made when the fulfillment of that prayer comes will bless beyond measure.*

The next excellent example of faith is found in Daniel Chapter 6. A brief summary of Daniel's story is that he prayed to God three times a day with his window open facing Jerusalem. King Darius favored Daniel, and jealous leaders in the kingdom developed a plan to trap Daniel. Those leaders had King Darius make a decree that no god except the king could be petitioned for a period of 30 days. Daniel, of course, continued his daily commitment and devotion to worship God. This was reported to the king and Daniel was thrown into the lions' den to be supposedly mauled and killed by the beasts.

However, that was not **God's** plan. Daniel was found safe in the lions' den the next day and the lions' mouths had been firmly shut by God! Daniel had **FAITH**! He *knew* that God would protect him.

I mentioned in my previous book, *Spiritual Growth: From Milk to Strong Meat*, about an organization I belonged to as a child. It was the Loyal Temperance Legion, and the motto we were taught was:

"DARE TO BE A DANIEL, DARE TO STAND ALONE, DARE TO MAKE A PROMISE TRUE, DARE TO MAKE IT KNOWN."

Through their teachings, coupled with what I learned from home and in church, I was saved at the age of nine.

Additionally, when I think about the motto from the Loyal Temperance Legion, my mind quickly went to the rainbow. Why, you may ask? Because that beautiful sign in the sky is the **promise** God gave to Noah after the great flood which covered the earth after 40 days and 40 nights of rain. *The scripture reference is found in Genesis 9:8-17.*

Worth the Journey: The Train Ride to Glory

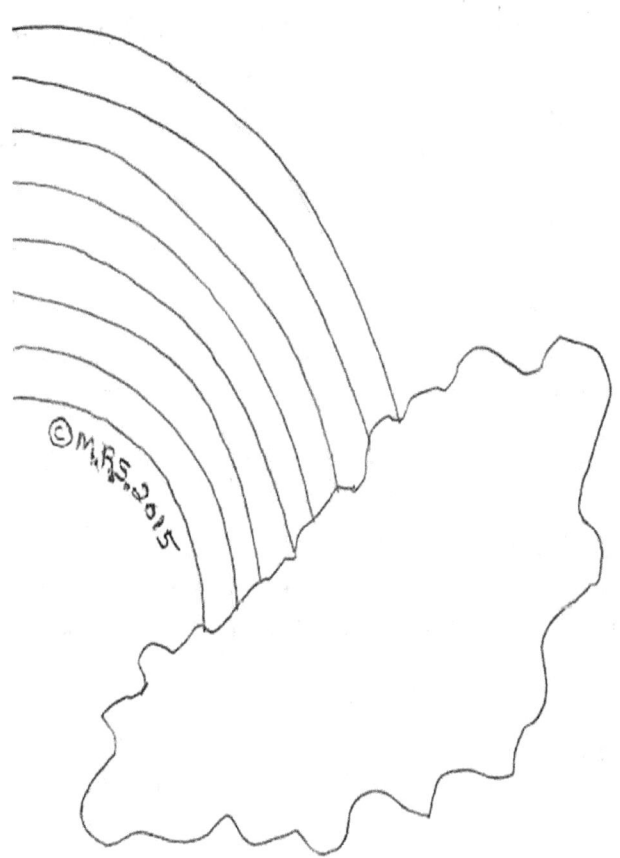

In doing a little research on the rainbow, I found it actually has **seven** colors and not the three- to five-color depictions we often see today in clothing, toys, and by social groups who may not know or care about the history and respect due that beautiful sign from God.

The seven colors are:

1. Red;
2. Orange;
3. Yellow;
4. Green;
5. Blue;
6. Indigo; and
7. Violet.

My spiritual thoughts went further to other significant sevens in the Bible, such as the seven days in a week and that the Sabbath is to be kept Holy.

Delving further into the Bible, we find in the Book of Revelations other sevens explained as "mysteries".

"The mystery of the seven stars which thou sawest in my right hand, and the seven golden candlesticks. The seven stars are the angels of the seven churches: and the seven candlesticks which thou sawest are the seven churches" (Revelation 1:20).

Worth the Journey: The Train Ride to Glory

No wonder some Christians consider the number seven to mean *completion*.

The *recommendation* here is to study and see for yourself the messages given – especially the characteristics of the seven churches – and see where your church is considered.

FAITH POWER POINT – *As with Daniel, faith **KNOWS** that God will protect His own in times of danger when they are **FAITHFUL** to Him.*

Finally, a little about Joseph the "Dreamer". The story begins in Genesis 37 when Joseph was 17 years old. His story shows many negative human situations he experienced – jealousy of brothers, being sold into slavery, false accusations, and being forgotten in prison – but God did not forget His faithful servant! In God's precise time, Joseph's interpreted dreams came true and saved the nation during years of famine. Eventually, a dream concerning his estranged brothers bowing down to him also came true when the brothers came seeking food. This family reunion caused Joseph to forgive the past injustices of the brothers, and the family received shelter and food during the crisis.

FAITH POWER POINT – *FAITH knows that trials may last a long time; but* **GOD** *never forgets His own and the final results are better than the initial situation.*

The hymn writer, Charles Wesley, penned many hymns still sung today in churches. The following portion of *Author of Faith, Eternal Word* contains a beautiful example:

> "By faith we know Thee strong to save;
> Save us, a present Savior Thou!
> Whate'er we hope, by faith we have
> Future and past subsisting now.
>
> "The things unknown to feeble sense,
> Unseen by reason's glimmering ray,
> With strong commanding evidence
> Their heavenly origin display.
>
> "Faith lends its realizing light,
> The clouds disperse, the shadows fly;
> The invisible appears in sight,
> And God is seen by mortal eye."

Worth the Journey: The Train Ride to Glory

Fruit of the Spirit

NEWBORN CHRISTIAN

FRUIT OF THE SPIRIT FACTS

1. *YOU MUST BE BORN AGAIN* to receive the Fruit of the Spirit!

2. All nine spiritual characteristics listed are "planted" in our souls at the time of conversion – salvation, believing in Jesus Christ, and becoming a member of the family of God.

3. It is not a plural word. Fruit is singular. Just like an orange or other fruit, there are several parts - but it is one item. The same applies to the *Fruit* of the Spirit. For example, an orange has seeds, pulp, sections, rind, stem, etc. Even the smallest seed is produced by each fruit, vegetable, flower, or tree. There are different parts while still being contained in its shell.

Worth the Journey: The Train Ride to Glory

Christians with the **Gift of Faith** may be considered visionary, able to imagine the unseen. To others, they may be dreamers like Joseph in the Old Testament. These individuals have the power to perceive something not present – the unknown and future things for the betterment of the Body of Christ.

Romans 4:17 comes to mind when calling things as if they are already existing:

"(As it is written, I have made thee a father of many nations,) before him whom he believed, even God, who quickeneth the dead, and calleth those things which be not as though they were."

In 1 Corinthians 12:8-10, we find that faith means to be firmly persuaded of God's power and promises to accomplish **His** will and **His** purpose, and to display such a confidence in **Him** and **His Word** that circumstances and obstacles do not shake that conviction. What a mouthful and depth of an explanation!

Jesus gives an example of a small mustard seed as a measure of faith. We are not necessarily speaking about the small, leafy vegetable eaten in salads or as a side dish. In biblical times, there was (and still is) in some areas the Sycamine tree which belongs to the Fig family. Some Bible versions refer to the tree as a *Sycamore*. Like most plant life, there are different varieties. According to research, there were two varieties of this large tree: one bearing sweet fruit and the other a bitter fruit. The tree has deep roots and is hard to kill. The Mulberry tree is a part of this tree family as well. The Sycamore tree is the one we are most familiar with in our times.

Worth the Journey: The Train Ride to Glory

"And the Lord said, "If ye had faith as a grain of mustard seed, ye might say unto this sycamine tree, "Be thou plucked up by the root, and be thou planted in the sea"; and it should obey you."
Luke 17:6

Mustard Tree (also Sycamine Tree)

(Read Jesus' parable of the Mustard Seed Tree in Matthew 13:31-32.)

I have found that often in the church body, members *assume* a person's education, vocational experiences, and family background qualify them to be the right choice for positions within the Christian church. That is not necessarily true.

The following statement must be noted, stressed, and taken heed of:

An individual's education, training, work experience, and vocation are NOT to be assumed as their SPIRITUAL GIFT.

An example may be a vocalist with a great voice in the *worldly/secular* setting. The individual, while being well-experienced and trained, may not have the anointed voice to be used in *God's* worship services. Another example includes educators from schools in the *public* setting who are not anointed to share the meanings and Christian love by teaching classes in *church*.

Worth the Journey: The Train Ride to Glory

MOUNTAINS IN MY LIFE THAT HAVING FAITH TO ENDURE CONQUERED

I firmly believe and know through faith that I can trust God's Word. All of my needs are supplied according to His riches in glory. No good thing does He withhold from me! I have indeed experienced hurts and pains throughout my journey. Some mountains in my life have been:

- Broken relationships;
- Deaths of parents;
- Taking responsibility for my mentally-challenged brother;
- Birth of a stillborn daughter after a difficult pregnancy;
- Insufficient funds to care for children alone;
- Job loss threatened with government downsizing; and
- Automobile repairs too expensive to have done.

Marlowe R. Scott

MOUNTAINS CONQUERED

Worth the Journey: The Train Ride to Glory

WAYS I CONTINUE TO GROW SPIRITUALLY AND OVERCOME MY MOUNTAINS

- I am blessed to read scriptures, have daily prayer, and read devotions throughout the day.
- I enjoy singing or humming spiritual songs/hymns out loud or rehearsing them in my mind.
- As Satan is the "Prince of the Air", speaking God's words out loud and singing those songs makes the devil cringe.
- I came from a nurturing Christian home with encouragement and positive reinforcement as I grew. Additionally, my church family and pastors were supportive of me and fostered growth in the church settings.

- No matter what people said or thought about me, I followed my parents' advice to always do my best. One of the sayings my mother repeated to me time and time again was, "You are no more important than anyone and no one is more important than you."
- With time, I learned the importance of laughing and not retaliating when others hurt me. I did not stoop to their level of ignorance.
- I learned self-respect and refused to act or be subservient to anyone - yet respectful to everyone. I practice the Bible teaching to do unto others as you would have them do unto you.
- I avoid negative personalities, people, and circumstances.

Worth the Journey: The Train Ride to Glory

- I was blessed with the Gift of Craftsmanship – although (admittedly) I did not *initially* recognize the source. This gift is referenced in Exodus 28:3 where God has filled with wisdom those to make Aaron's priestly garments.

The Gift of *Wisdom* is found in James 3:17

"But the wisdom that is from above is first pure, then peaceable, gentle, and easy to be intreated, full of mercy and good fruits without partiality and without hypocrisy."

BE POWERFUL: TAKE ACTION!
What new faith concept have you learned that has strengthened your Christian journey?

Worth the Journey: The Train Ride to Glory

The Fruit of the Spirit has nine qualities. Which are your prominent ones and which do you need to pray over and develop?

_____

_____

_____

_____

_____

_____

_____

_____

_____

_____

_____

_____

How and where do you use your Spiritual Gifts?

_____

_____

_____

_____

_____

_____

_____

_____

_____

_____

_____

_____

_____

JESUS' ASCENSION AND GIFTS

When Jesus ascended to His Father in Heaven, He gave gifts to men besides those given by the Fruit of the Spirit at conversion.

"Wherefore He saith, when He ascended up on high, He led captivity captive, and gave gifts unto men."

Ephesians 4:8

Examples of those Spiritual Gifts may be found in the following scriptures:

- Romans 12 - exhortation, giving, leadership, mercy, prophecy, service, and teaching.
- 1 Corinthians 12 – administration, apostle, discernment, faith, healing, helps, knowledge, miracles, prophecy, teaching, tongues, interpretation of tongues, and wisdom.
- Ephesians 4 - apostle, evangelism, pastor, prophecy, and teaching.

- Other passages give the gifts of celibacy, hospitality, martyrdom, missionary, and voluntary poverty.

- 2 Peter 1:5-8 provides excellent scriptural advice:

  "And beside this, giving all diligence, add to your faith virtue; and to virtue knowledge;
  "And to knowledge temperance; and to temperance patience; and to patience godliness;
  "And to godliness brotherly kindness; and to brotherly kindness charity.
  "For if these things be in you, and abound, they make you that ye shall neither be barren nor unfruitful in the knowledge of our Lord Jesus Christ."

Faith and references to it are made throughout Scripture. Once again, Scripture from the Book of Revelations is pertinent. Revelations 21:1-6 clearly states we are to be **faithful unto death** and the **reward** will be a ***crown of life*** (meaning eternal life) in Heaven with God! This passage is often quoted at home-going (funeral) services.

> *"And I saw a new heaven and a new earth: for the first heaven and the first earth were passed away; and there was no more sea.*
> *"And I John saw the holy city, new Jerusalem, coming down from God out of heaven, prepared as a bride adorned for her husband.*

Worth the Journey: The Train Ride to Glory

> *"And I heard a great voice out of heaven saying, Behold, the tabernacle of God is with men, and he will dwell with them, and they shall be his people, and God himself shall be with them, and be their God.*
>
> *"And God shall wipe away all tears from their eyes; and there shall be no more death, neither sorrow, nor crying, neither shall there be any more pain: for the former things are passed away.*
>
> *"And he that sat upon the throne said, Behold, I make all things new. And he said unto me, Write: for these words are true and faithful.*
>
> *"And he said unto me, It is done. I am Alpha and Omega, the beginning and the end. I will give unto him that is athirst of the fountain of the Water of Life freely."*

Just the assurance of *all* things being made new, that God's words are true and *faithful*, and that the fountain of the Water of Life is for *us* brings me great joy! To this promise, I can only say **"ALLELUIA!"**

Marlowe R. Scott

Living Waters

ADDENDUM
"THE ABUSIVE AND UNRULY TONGUE"

"Even so the tongue is a little member,

and boasteth great things.

Behold, how great a matter a

Little fire kindleth!"

James 3:5

Marlowe R. Scott

This last chapter addresses the subject of abuse. Pearly Gates Publishing LLC placed a call for individuals to share their personal stories of abuse - past or present. The title of the book series is *God Says I Am Battle-Scar Free: Testimonies of Abuse Survivors*.

While my input into the book is what some may consider a "light" form of abuse, it nevertheless **can** and **does** hurt - causing irreparable damage. It is presented in *this* book for several reasons, to include: the sharing of an inspirational poem; how my **faith** in Jesus Christ helped me during those times; and to encourage others to overcome this damaging form of abuse.

Almost immediately after being asked to share my story in Pearly Gates Publishing LLC's collaboration, I had the *strong* desire to write a poem for the book. As most of my poetry comes as a spurt of inspiration from God, I was not receiving any words.

God revealed Himself in a **mighty** way on my 71st Birthday: July 16, 2015. That morning (and within the usual 15 to 20 minutes), the following poem came to me! What a blessing and, at the same time, humbling birthday present!

Worth the Journey: The Train Ride to Glory

Some instances of abuse are misrepresented to be in the "name of love", thus the title *Abuse is Not Love* was chosen.

Marlowe R. Scott

ABUSE IS NOT LOVE
Marlowe R. Scott © 2015

Abuse comes in many forms.
In some cultures and homes,
Abuse is the norm.
It's directed at children and adults, too;
Has abuse ever happened to you?
Have scars – seen and unseen –
Impacted this earthly life?
Have loved-ones inflicted pains causing deep strife?
What to do? Where to turn for relief?
Will anyone believe my deepening grief?
There has to be a way to make it through another day.
Help me, Dear Lord; Help me I pray.
I have heard about Jesus
And how He came to save us.
Is Jesus the answer for me?
If so, this is my plea.
Help me, Dear Jesus.
Help me right now.
At your throne I throw my cares and humbly bow.
Please relieve the pain; make it go away.
I believe you can, and this I pray:
"Thank you for the warm comfort I now feel.
Thank you, Dear Jesus, because I know you can heal.
Take my abuser under your care,
So that no one else will feel the pains I bear."

Worth the Journey: The Train Ride to Glory

By definition, abuse has many forms and degrees of harm – much too numerous for exploring here. Today's world has even found new ways to abuse others (i.e. cyber-bullying). The word itself may be defined as:

- Misuse;
- To treat badly;
- To hurt with words;
- Degradation;
- Injustice;
- Damage;
- Impair;
- Nag;
- Victimize; and
- Knock about.

The "tongue" is a small member of the human body, yet it can cause great and lifelong damage to anyone! Some people, including slave-owners, husbands, and preachers misinterpret scriptures to control, subdue, degrade, and otherwise use others to their advantage.

Marlowe R. Scott

There are many sayings I heard when growing up, such as "Loose lips sink ships" and (during my 1950's and 60's youth) "Sticks and stones may break my bones, but words will never hurt me". I was instructed to just walk away from taunting whenever possible. *Things have changed drastically!*

Worth the Journey: The Train Ride to Glory

Daily in the news, there are instances of injury and even death caused by family members, neighbors, and authorities over words.

Critical areas which may not be readily considered are those words from parents and guardians which greatly impact their children. It is wise to heed the words found in the Book of Ephesians 6:4: *"And, ye fathers, provoke not your children to wrath: but bring them up in the nurture and admonition of the Lord."* Colossians 3:21 states, *"Fathers, provoke not your children to anger, lest they be discouraged."* It is important to note here that on occasion, those negative qualities expressed through words also occur in educational settings.

The Holy Bible has **many** passages and verses which teach truths about the tongue. Those verses are my source for true and unwavering guidance in *many* situations.

A few verses follow. Please take time to slowly read them, absorb the message, and let them speak to you:

- Proverbs 10:19 – *"In the multitude of words there wanteth not sin: but he that refraineth his lips is wise."*

- Proverbs 12:18 – *"There is that speaketh like the piercings of a sword: but the tongue of the wise is health."*

- Isaiah 59:3 – *"For your hands are defiled with blood, and your fingers with iniquity; your lips have spoken lies, your tongue hath muttered perverseness."*

- James 1:6 – *"And the tongue is a fire, a world of iniquity: so is the tongue among our members, that it defileth the whole body, and setteth on fire the course of nature; and it is set on fire of hell."*

- James 1:26 – *"If any man among you seem to be religious, and bridleth not his tongue, but deceiveth his own heart, this man's religion is vain."*

Worth the Journey: The Train Ride to Glory

PERSONAL INSTANCES HOW WORDS HURT ME

Instance #1

Around the age of eight, I joined the Girl Scout Brownies in our country town of primarily Caucasians. At one of the meetings, a girl called another Caucasian member the "N" word. She quickly showed that she had regretted the remark and the other girls looked at her with shock. *It is important to note that once words (or even **one** word) are spoken out loud, they cannot be retrieved.* Think before you speak.

After leaving the meeting, I went home and told my mother I did not want to belong to the troop any longer. I refused to tell her *why*. The damage had already been done.

Marlowe R. Scott

Instance #2

During my junior high school years, I entered 9th grade at 225 pounds. At the time, the song "16 Tons" was popular. Some cruel classmates would call me by that name. Initially it hurt, but in time I learned to smile and the taunting gradually stopped. However, I must tell you that by the time I graduated high school, I was a well-formed 140 pounds on my 5' 7" frame and many - especially the males - regretted they had spoken ill of me during my high school years.

NOTE: *As I have gotten older, weight has been gained, and my limbs and joints pain; however, my self-respect, personality, positive attitude, and Godly-wisdom* **still** *draw others to me.*

Worth the Journey: The Train Ride to Glory

Instance #3

Even in the church, I was deeply hurt and spiritually-abused by words. As it is in many churches, there was a rule that choir members come to practice before singing on their assigned Sunday. One particular Sunday, I was in the basement of the small church helping with the Sunday school session. I was able to hear the choir upstairs going over the songs for the 11:00 am service. *It must be mentioned that they were rehearsing familiar hymns.*

After Sunday school was over, a faithful older teacher routinely put on her choir robe and went upstairs to sing. She encouraged me to come up with her. She *assured* me that it would be fine to come, so I put on my robe and followed her.

As I was ascending the steps to the choir box, the organist stopped me. She told me I could not sing because I was not at choir practice. I tried to explain that I was downstairs with the children, but that I heard the practice and knew the hymns. She insisted that I leave the choir. I walked back down the middle aisle with tears in my eyes, went outside the sanctuary, sat down, and wept.

After I was better composed, I asked the ushers to get my young children from the sanctuary and we went home. The hurt was deeper than I could ever have imagined. The pastor, officers, and members called me after they found out what had occurred and tried to console me, but it did not ease the pain. In time, I found another church closer to my home and worshipped there for many years.

Before ending the sharing of *this* experience, I must add: Guess what? In time, the same organist joined the church where I had become a member! Another saying and truth from my mother: *"Don't be a church-jumper. There are people-problems in every church."* While that saying did not apply directly to me, it is true. People make up the church membership, and there are many who need to be saved, grow, and be healed.

Worth the Journey: The Train Ride to Glory

As stated earlier, hymns, spirituals, and gospel songs bring me great comfort. The following song came to me one evening. It is a familiar hymn, *O For a Thousand Tongues to Sing*, written by Charles Wesley. Following are the first four verses of this beautiful hymn. The words speak of triumphs, the calming of fears, and cleansing by the Blood of Jesus.

1. O for a thousand tongues to sing
   my great Redeemer's praise,
   the glories of my God and King,
   the triumphs of his grace!
2. My gracious Master and my God,
   assist me to proclaim,
   to spread through all the earth abroad
   the honors of thy name.
3. Jesus! The name that charms our fears,
   that bids our sorrows cease;
   'tis music in the sinner's ears,
   'tis life, and health, and peace.
4. He breaks the power of canceled sin,
   he sets the prisoner free;
   his blood can make the foulest clean;
   his blood availed for me.

Marlowe R. Scott

Because of my personal experience and experiences others have shared concerning choirs and church music, this final sharing is about my sincere innermost beliefs about music in God's sanctuary and elsewhere. Those singing should believe the words they sing! If not, their singing does not - I repeat, **DOES NOT** - glorify or edify God! It is just someone with a good voice singing a song.

I once knew a woman (she is now deceased) who often sang in church using different tempos, words that were not part of the original song, and other subtle differences some people might notice; **BUT** when she began worshipping with her voice, the congregation would feel the Holy Spirit, people would rejoice, and this woman's anointing from God was *clearly* evident.

A choir that I was president of used to march in on the words of *We Have Come This Far By Faith* which has now been enhanced by some musicians to include *I Will Trust In the Lord*. What a stirring those words bring to my *soul*!

Worth the Journey: The Train Ride to Glory

Before ending this experience about the choir and church music, I feel it is imperative that biblical documentation be shared about who Satan was in Heaven *before* being cast out by God.

He was a *musical angel*. By understanding his beauty, valuable gems, and musical instruments (tambourine-type small drum and pipes), it is easy to understand why some churches split because of dissension and trouble in the choir or why some choir leaders and organists are more into themselves than into their purpose within the Body of Christ.

Satan is known by many names and descriptive characteristics:

- Abaddon;
- Tempter;
- Apollyon;
- Accuser;
- Father of Lies;
- Adversary;
- Angel of the Abyss; and
- Beelzebub - to share a few.

In Ephesians 2:2, he is referred to as "Ruler of the Kingdom of the Air". That should give **everyone** something to think about with all the cyber-crimes and diseases we have on earth transmitted through the *air*.

The prophet Ezekiel describes the King of Tyrus (Tyre). As I have read the entire bible, that, too, was read, but without understanding the full message. Bible study classes made it clearer and (prayerfully) will help others understand.

Ezekiel 28:11-19

"Moreover the word of the LORD came unto me, saying,
"Son of man, take up a lamentation upon the king of Tyrus, and say unto him, Thus saith the Lord GOD; Thou sealest up the sum, full of wisdom, and perfect in beauty.
"Thou hast been in Eden the garden of God; every precious stone was thy covering, the sardius, topaz, and the diamond, the beryl, the onyx, and the jasper, the sapphire, the emerald, and the carbuncle, and gold: the workmanship of thy tabrets and of thy pipes was prepared in thee in the day that thou wast created.

Worth the Journey: The Train Ride to Glory

"Thou art the anointed cherub that covereth; and I have set thee so: thou wast upon the holy mountain of God; thou hast walked up and down in the midst of the stones of fire.

"Thou wast perfect in thy ways from the day that thou wast created, till iniquity was found in thee.

"By the multitude of thy merchandise they have filled the midst of thee with violence, and thou hast sinned: therefore I will cast thee as profane out of the mountain of God: and I will destroy thee, O covering cherub, from the midst of the stones of fire.

"Thine heart was lifted up because of thy beauty, thou hast corrupted thy wisdom by reason of thy brightness: I will cast thee to the ground, I will lay thee before kings, that they may behold thee.

"Thou hast defiled thy sanctuaries by the multitude of thine iniquities, by the iniquity of thy traffick; therefore will I bring forth a fire from the midst of thee, it shall devour thee, and I will bring thee to ashes upon the earth in the sight of all them that behold thee.

"All they that know thee among the people shall be astonished at thee: thou shalt be a terror, and never shalt thou be any more."

BE POWERFUL: TAKE ACTION!

Have you had an experience of being abused by someone's tongue or in another manner? If so, how did that experience make you feel?

Worth the Journey: The Train Ride to Glory

What steps did you take to overcome the experience?

_____

_____

_____

_____

_____

_____

_____

_____

_____

_____

_____

_____

_____

_____

There are suggestions presented in the abuse section on how to find comfort after abuse occurs. Add ways that may work for you.

_____

_____

_____

_____

_____

_____

_____

_____

_____

_____

_____

_____

CONCLUSION

- Remain faithful to our Faithful Savior, Jesus Christ.
- Heaven is the Christian's goal. Jesus suffered and died to make it a **HOME** for us! *Remember*: God knows every hair on your head and cares for you (see Matthew 10:30).
- Read and meditate on comforting Scriptures.
- Pray for strength from God as trials come and as they continue. **PRAISE HIM** even in the valleys (see Psalm 23)!
- Remember testimonies from the Holy Bible and attend a Bible-preaching, Bible-believing church. Listen to others who have overcome their trials. Share your testimonies as well.
- Our faithfulness found in our belief in God and through salvation **NEVER** ends. He is always with us, **NEVER** stops loving us, and forgives our many trespasses and sins when we truly repent.

Marlowe R. Scott

The following scripture is offered to conclude this short story on the tongue:

"A wholesome tongue is a tree of life:

but perverseness therein is a breach in the

spirit."

Proverbs15:4

Worth the Journey: The Train Ride to Glory

Closing Prayer for the Reader

Dear Heavenly Father of all mankind who knows every thought and action before we do, may each one reading this book have a Spiritual Spark ignited to use those gifts and Fruit of the Spirit you have given. For those who have not realized the value of these gifts, may they discover and become dedicated to using theirs to edify the Body of Christ. With the acknowledgment of these gifts, may they take their role in spreading the Gospel of Jesus Christ through the Great Commission given to the Saved in Matthew 28:18-20:

"And Jesus came and spake unto them, saying, All power is given unto me in heaven and in earth.
"Go ye therefore, and teach all nations, baptizing them in the name of the Father, and of the Son, and of the Holy Ghost:
"Teaching them to observe all things whatsoever I have commanded you: and, lo, I am with you always, even unto the end of the world. Amen."

Marlowe R. Scott

REFERENCES FOR SPIRITUAL GIFTS INVENTORY/ASSESSMENT

- www.umc.org/what-we-believe/spiritual-gifts
- www.buildingchurch.net/g2s.htm

Note: Christian bookstores have resource materials as well. For those wishing additional resources, type the words Spiritual Gift Inventory or Spiritual Gift Assessment in the search engine of your Internet browser.

NATIONAL DOMESTIC ABUSE RESOURCES

- National Domestic Violence Hotline
  Staffed 24 hours a day by trained counselors who can provide crisis assistance and information about shelters, legal advocacy, health care centers, and counselling.
  1-800-799-SAFE (7233)
  1-800-787-3224 (TDD)

- Faith Trust Institute
  (Formerly the Center for the Prevention of Sexual and Domestic Violence)
  2400 N. 45th Street, #10
  Seattle, WA 98103
  Phone: 206-634-1903, ext. 10
  Email: info@faithtrustinstitute.org

Dedication

This book is dedicated to all Christians making the journey to the Cross leading to our Heavenly Home and to those yet to be saved who will join in the journey.

Acknowledgments

Always giving praises and thanks to our Lord and Savior Jesus Christ for all He continues to do in my life and the lives of others touched through the gifts given to me.

To my daughter, Angela R. Edwards, the CEO of Pearly Gates Publishing, LLC: Much love for your continued ministry through using your many talents to uplift God's Kingdom.

For those who have taken the time to provide endorsements and words of encouragement, I sincerely **THANK EACH OF YOU.** May this book also provide spiritual nourishment to you and those you touch.

Marlowe R. Scott

A Special Note from President Obama & Family

In September 2015, President Barak Obama and family were given an autographed copy of Spiritual Growth: From Milk to Strong Meat, the first book that became an Amazon Best Seller. The Obamas sent a note of appreciation stating in part:

> *"Thank you for your gift. It was such a nice gesture, and we were touched by your generosity. Your thoughtfulness reflects the extraordinary kindness of the American people. More than anything, please know that your kind words and support for our shared values motivate us each and every day."*

Worth the Journey: The Train Ride to Glory

Preface

The writing of *Keeping It Real: The Straight and Narrow* could not be written without remembering a special evangelist I worshipped with for many years. She possessed many genuine Christian qualities within my view, with the primary being godly wisdom. She ardently studied scriptures, mentored many, possessed a spirit of humbleness, taught God's Word clearly, and preached deep truths without wavering.

That special human vessel regularly spoke about "unction"- a word you may not hear too often today. Unction is the act of anointing as a sign of consecration; also a soothing ointment; a manner indicating or arousing emotion, especially religious fervor. She always had oil with her for anointing, would willingly pray for anyone anywhere at any time, and was highly respected by ministers who listened to and used her wise counsel.

She was a regular teacher at Black Rock Retreat Center, Quarryville, Pennsylvania in Lancaster County where we experienced many mountaintop experiences together. Although she has gone on to her Heavenly reward, she has left a legacy that will live on in those lives she touched. She constantly emphasized being "real" and that people must stop "playing church".

Worth the Journey: The Train Ride to Glory

Introduction

The inspiration and title for this book were given to me in September 2015. *Keeping It Real: The Straight and Narrow* has been a spiritual work in progress (so to speak) as is our journey to our Heavenly Home. The cross depicted on the front cover aptly represents the Cross bore on Calvary by our Lord and Savior, Jesus Christ.

There is a well-loved and widely sung hymn of the church, *The Old Rugged Cross* by George Bennard, the words of which resonate deep in my soul as I sing or hum them. All verses and chorus are shared here, as they have deep meanings and truths for "Real" believers in Jesus Christ.

Old Rugged Cross
By: George Bennard

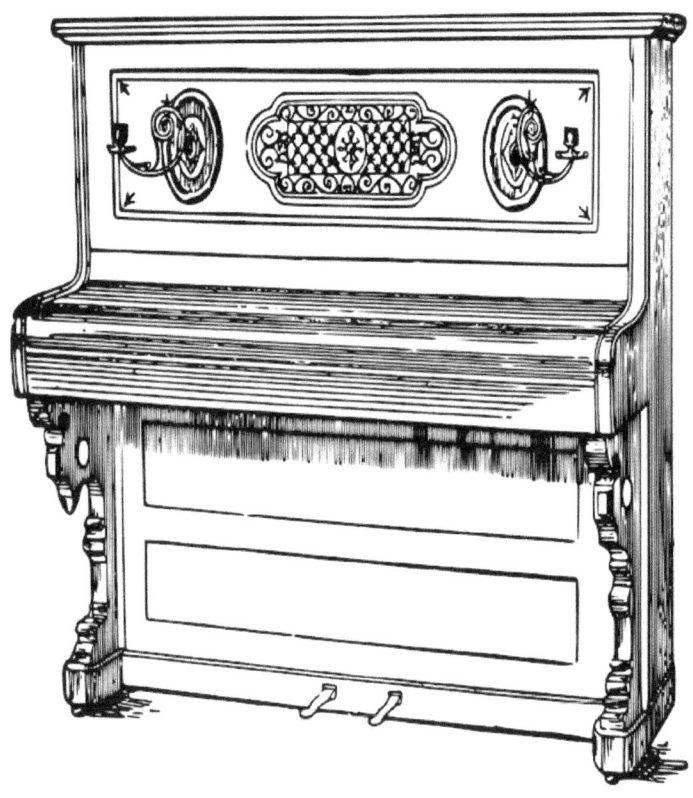

Worth the Journey: The Train Ride to Glory

Old Rugged Cross

On a hill far away stood an old rugged cross,
The emblem of suffering and shame;
And I love that old cross where the dearest and best
For a world of lost sinners was slain.

CHORUS:
So I'll cherish the old rugged cross,
Till my trophies at last I lay down;
I will cling to the old rugged cross,
And exchange it some day for a crown.

O that old rugged cross, so despised by the world,
Has a wondrous attraction for me;
For the dear Lamb of God left his glory above
To bear it to dark Calvary.

In that old rugged cross, stained with blood so divine,
A wondrous beauty I see,
For 'twas on that old rugged cross Jesus suffered and died,
To pardon and sanctify me.

To that old rugged cross I will ever be true,
Its shame and reproach gladly bear;
Then he'll call me some day to my home far away,
Where his glory forever I'll share.

Marlowe R. Scott

Note: *When I was married in 2006, Rev. Richard W. Jones suggested using our beautiful main sanctuary at Tabernacle Baptist Church in Burlington, New Jersey. I told him I wanted to get married in the chapel, which was a part of the older church. It was intimate and has a rugged cross suspended in the front. This represented what my heart desired and we were married there. Sometime before getting married, an evangelist I had known for some time told me the story of how the cross came to be. It was created by Richard A. Timbers, Sr. He would collect driftwood from the nearby Delaware River in Burlington, New Jersey and create beautiful works of art.*

In preparing to write this book, I was inspired at my kitchen table to include the uplifting hymn *How to Reach the Masses* (also known as *Lift Him Up*). In checking a familiar website I use to gather background information, I discovered an amazing fact! The composer of this popular hymn was Johnson Oatman, Jr. who was born April 21, 1856 near Medford, New Jersey - which is only 20 minutes from my home! I was so excited, I called friends and relatives with my new knowledge.

Worth the Journey: The Train Ride to Glory

Mr. Oatman was a member of a Methodist church, became an Ordained Minister, and is credited with **thousands** of compositions! Other well-known hymns credited to him are: Count Your Blessings, Higher Ground (also known as I'm Pressing On the Upward Way), No, Not One, and The Last Mile of the Way.

For our local Burlington County New Jersey residents, we know individuals who attended the New Jersey Collegiate Institute in Bordentown - as did Mr. Oatman. He married Wilhelminia Reid and had three children: Rachel, Miriam, and Percy. Johnson Oatman, Jr. died September 25, 1922 at the age of 66.

Two of Mr. Oatman's hymns are included in this book. For those who know the melodies, why not pause and sing or hum to yourself as you meditate on and soak in the words? That is what I do frequently. I find peace and comfort in both the words **and** melody.

Marlowe R. Scott

Lift Him Up
By: Johnson Oatman, Jr.

Worth the Journey: The Train Ride to Glory

Lift Him Up

How to reach the masses, men of every birth,
For an answer, Jesus gave the key:
"And I, if I be lifted up from the earth,
Will draw all men unto Me."

Refrain:
Lift Him up, lift Him up;
Still He speaks from eternity;
"And I, if I be lifted up from the earth,
Will draw all men unto Me."

Oh! The world is hungry for the Living Bread,
Lift the Savior up for them to see;
Trust Him, and do not doubt the words that He said,
"I'll draw all men unto me."

Don't exalt the preacher, don't exalt the pew,
Preach the Gospel simple, full, and free;
Prove Him and you will find that promise is true,
"I'll draw all men unto Me."

Lift Him up by living as a Christian ought,
Let the world in you the Savior see;
Then men will gladly follow Him Who once taught,
"I'll draw all men unto Me."

As you read, contemplate, and digest the message of this book, may it inspire you and improve your relationship with Jesus as here on Earth, we strive - step by step up our personal mountains - to reach our Heavenly Home.

You are encouraged to make notes and respond to the questions at the end of each chapter. They are there to remind you of times when you may have been blessed and inspired, as well as to share your thoughts with others.

This book moves along the journey one must travel on the **'Straight and Narrow'** through the sharing of scriptures, stories, illustrations, and poems. May you come to know (as I have) the dry and rough places on the journey ultimately end. The lessons learned become testimonies and evidence of Jesus' unending love for us until we meet Him face to face.

Worth the Journey: The Train Ride to Glory

KEY SCRIPTURES

*"The voice of him that crieth in the wilderness,
prepare ye the way
of the Lord, make straight in the desert a highway for
our God.
Every valley shall be exalted, and every mountain and
hill shall be made low: and the crooked shall be made
straight, and the rough places plain:
And the glory of the Lord shall be revealed, and all
flesh shall see it together: for the mouth of the Lord
hath spoken it."*

Isaiah 40:3-5

*"Enter ye in at the strait gate: for wide is the gate,
and broad is the way, that leadeth to destruction, and
many there be
which go in thereat:
Because strait is the gate, and narrow is the way,
which leadeth
unto life, and few there be that find it."*

Matthew 7:13-14

Marlowe R. Scott

CHAPTER ONE
KEEPING IT REAL

Worth the Journey: The Train Ride to Glory

What does "real" mean? It is something true, actual, genuine, authentic, and sincere. "Narrow" is defined as a path or way with a little 'wiggle room' to go left, right, or to even do a complete turn around. In the context of this writing, the "Real Narrow" way leads to life – **eternal life**.

I admit: There are paths in life which may be wider and easier to humanly travel, but those paths do not lead to the Cross of Calvary and eternal life. The wider paths may include such things associated with wayward friendships, hang-ups, greed, habits, and those sins and wrongs set out clearly in the Holy Scriptures.

There are many imitations in today's world that look like and appear to be the real thing:

- Furs
- Leather coats and handbags
- Jewelry
- Imitation foods - i.e. butter and sugar
- Artificial turf on sports fields
- Imitation flavorings
- Building materials - i.e. marble, brick, and wood - that appear real.

Likewise, sometimes during church worship, some unreal things may occur. Scripture addresses them clearly in the speaking of vain words, religious traditions and rituals instituted by man, judging others by their outward appearance or circumstance, and singing songs without believing or applying those words to our lives.

There may also be other reasons, such as those who imitate what others do and feel that is the way to worship. There could be newly-converted Christians in the midst who do not yet understand how to interpret and apply scripture to resist the numerous temptations of the world and deceptions of the devil.

I heard some time ago that the higher our spiritual level becomes, the harder the devil tries to tempt and hinder our journey. For those who read my previous book, *Believing Without Seeing: The Power of Faith*, you are familiar with and have read the addendum at the end about Satan, the fallen angel cast out of Heaven by God.

Worth the Journey: The Train Ride to Glory

Questions for Consideration

1. When you have perceived "unreal" things in church, how have you ignored them and remained focused on the worship service?

2. How have religious traditions hindered your growth and understanding of true worship?

CHAPTER TWO
THE DEVIL GOES TO CHURCH

Marlowe R. Scott

As shared in prior writings, my mother had many talents and was often invited to sing or recite poetry in church as well as civic programs. The reading of the following poem was requested **many** times. It is from a collection of poetry entitled *Alabaster Boxes* by Bessie Brent Winston (copyrighted in 1947).

The poem's title is *The Devil Goes to Church*. It shows qualities and temptations presented to ourselves and others as we travel our personal path to the cross. The poem is written in a form known as 'satire', which effectively uses humor to show weaknesses, bad qualities, and sarcasm to make its point.

Worth the Journey: The Train Ride to Glory

THE DEVIL GOES TO CHURCH

The devil went to church one day,
And as he strolled along
He planned how he could execute
Some deeds of sin and wrong.
He did not stop down near the door,
As most outsiders would,
But went as close as he could get
To where the preacher stood.

He heard him read in earnest tones
Words from the Holy Book;
The devil turned and hurled at him
An ugly, angry look.
He heard him tell with gentle voice
The curse of sin and pain,
And strive to bring the straying sheep
Back to the fold again.

He heard him tell in wisdom's words
Salvation's wondrous plan.
The devil frowned and bit his lip
And said, "I hate that man.
I've done my best by day and night
To lead this flock astray;
He'll undo everything I've done,
If he goes on this way."

Marlowe R. Scott

So down the aisle he made his way
To see what he could do
Along the line of starting things
And making trouble brew.
He saw two girls down near the door,
With faces sweet and fair,
With heads bowed low, as if they were
In earnest, thoughtful prayer.

Straight to those girls the devil went
And said, "Look at that hat
That Sister Molly Gray has on,
And Easter day at that!"
Then up from thoughts of prayer and praise
Two pair of roguish eyes
Went straight to Sister Molly's hat
In mischievous surprise.

And then they bowed their heads again
And laughed and giggled till
The deacon had to go to them
And ask them to be still.
And then the devil took a seat
By Sister Mary Wood;
He knew she'd much prefer to hear
The bad instead of good.

Worth the Journey: The Train Ride to Glory

He whispered something in her ear,
And then she turned her head
And whispered to the deacon's wife,
I don't know what she said,
But instantly the deacon's wife
Replied, "O dear, O dear,
If that is true, then I'll not pay
Another penny here."

The devil grinned and went his way,
His joy too deep to tell,
And as he went he murmured low,
"That worked out pretty well."
And then he went to Brother Green -
He'd seen him yawn and gap.
He said, "Just lean your head on me,
And take a little nap."

He gently rocked him to and fro
Down dreamland's pathway steep
And sang him impish lullabies
Till he was fast asleep.
He saw a small boy passing by,
On some dire mischief bent;
Then down the aisle and through the door
A wireless was sent.

Marlowe R. Scott

It read like this: "Peep in the door
At good old Silas Blair;
He'll kneel in just a little while
To make a silly prayer.
Just keep an eye, and when he does,
You throw a stone and run.
It won't be wrong, for every boy
Must have a little fun."

And so it happened that a stone
Came whizzing through the air
And made poor Brother Silas jump
And yell out in despair.
An Amen brother, stanch and true,
Whose name was Aaron Kent,
Had in his worn-out pocketbook
A dollar and a cent.

He hadn't been to church for months,
And so had planned to spare
The dollar bill to sort of pay
For times he wasn't there.
The devil sat down by his side
And whispered in his ear,
"You're just as crazy as a bat
To pay that dollar here.

Worth the Journey: The Train Ride to Glory

"The church clerk and the treasurer, too,
Are crooked as can be,
They always take their spending change
From out of the treasury.
Where do you think the treasurer's wife
Gets all her fancy clothes?
She never does a lick of work,
But dresses up and goes.

"That clerk has got a brand new car,
All shiny, black and sleek;
Folks don't go in for cars like that
On twenty-five per week.
So take your dollar bill straight home
And put your penny in;
To help those crooked folks along
Would really be a sin."

So when the plate was passed around,
Good Brother Aaron Kent
Kept back the nice new dollar bill
And gave the church the cent.
The devil smacked him on the back
And said, "That's fine, old dear,
And don't you ever, ever give
More than a penny here."

Marlowe R. Scott

A little girl named Rosabelle,
  Who came from Tennessee,
Was chairman of a junior club
  They called The Busy Bee.
The club had labored faithfully
  Through each hot summer day,
Till twenty-four bright bills
  In their small treasury lay.

The devil said to Rosabelle,
  "That hat at Kimberly's
Has been reduced to four-nineteen;
  It's pretty as can be.
Why don't you go and get that hat
  Before Jane Spencer does?
She always thinks she looks so nice;
  Don't hesitate, because

"Part of that money's yours by rights;
  You worked just like a mule;
To give the church the whole of it,
  You'd be a little fool."
And so on next church meeting day,
  The lovely Rosabelle
Was dressed up in a brand new hat,
  And purse and gloves as well.

Worth the Journey: The Train Ride to Glory

He found his way up in the choir,
Where only peace belongs,
And sitting down cross-legged, went
To meddling with the song
He whispered in a sister's ear,
"This isn't fair a bit;
Unless they sang the hymns I liked,
If I were you, I'd quit.

And then an ugly selfish look
Came in that sister's eyes,
And made the organist look up
In sad and grave surprise.
He made the tenors laugh and talk
Till there was not a trace
Of order in the choir stand;
It bordered on disgrace.

He then walked up and down the aisle
And looked at everyone,
To see if there was anything
That he had left undone.
He really wasn't satisfied;
He could have spent the day,
Rejoicing in his devilment
And leading folks astray.

Marlowe R. Scott

The sermon being over now,
The devil got his hat
And said, "I wish I'd had more time,
But 'twasn't bad at that."
And when he snuggled down to sleep,
His imps all heard him say,
"I'm tired as a man can be,
But what a happy day!"

~ The End ~

Worth the Journey: The Train Ride to Glory

Questions for Consideration

1. I have personally done some of those things cited in this poem, from youth to adulthood. How has this poem made you more aware of doing the same things in church?

_____

_____

_____

_____

_____

_____

_____

_____

_____

_____

_____

2. What do you feel is the overall message of this poem?

CHAPTER THREE
MOUNTAIN CLIMBING

In preparing to climb mountains on Earth, you need the correct footwear, ropes, walking sticks, backpack, food, and water - to name a *few* essentials. During the ascent, you may encounter slippery rocks, streams, waterfalls, caves, briers, snakes, stinging insects, and wild animals. Along the way, there may also be welcomed plateaus for rest or insurmountable obstacles.

For the climb we must take on our **spiritual** journey, we also need supplies and weapons to combat snares, hardships, hurts, and pains we face. Spiritual armor for this type of mountain climbing and battle is found in Ephesians 6:10-18. A fuller discussion on that passage of scripture was presented in my first publication, *Spiritual Growth: From Milk to Strong Meat*, and also shares valuable information learned from a class on Spiritual Warfare. God has provided spiritual armor for us. To stay battle-ready, we must study scriptures, pray, hear Christ-centered preaching, worship God, and fellowship regularly with believers while learning how to apply and use what God has given us for combat!

Worth the Journey: The Train Ride to Glory

For *seasoned* Christians, you may identify with the journey to the Cross of Calvary. For *newer* Christians, they will learn that trials, temptations, and worldly turmoil will happen, but be assured: Jesus will be with you every step you take and with each burden you bear.

In the New Testament, Jesus illustrated many truths through His telling of parables. A brief definition of a parable is that it is a short story teaching a spiritual or moral lesson or truth. For the following story, there is a literary term called an 'allegory' which represents a quality or idea in the likeness of a person or thing, to be interpreted *symbolically*.

Such is the story I read years ago: *The Pilgrim's Progress*. It tells the experience of the main character, Christian, striving to reach the Celestial City - his Heavenly destination. Following is a brief summary.

Marlowe R. Scott

THE PILGRIM'S PROGRESS
John Bunyan (written 1678)

The story has several terms Christians may be able to identify with. The main character is Christian. He started the journey to the Celestial City (also called Mount Zion). He had to make the journey alone because his family would not accompany him. He went through such places and the "Slough of Despondent", "Valley to Humiliation", "Valley of the Shadow of Death", and mountains of "Error and Caution". He, at one point, is sheltered in 'Goodwill's' home where he learns about faith. He also meets three 'Shining Ones' and four mistresses of the 'Palace Beautiful' who shelter him and give him weapons.

Along the way, he encounters Apollyon and uses a sword to ward him off. The story continues through others' personal encounters, to include 'Shepherds' who inform him that others have died trying to reach the Celestial City and warned him to be aware of shortcuts which may actually be paths to Hell. Christian finally reaches the Land of Beulah along with a companion he picked up earlier, but they must cross a river. With some struggles, they make it safely across and are welcomed into the Celestial City by its residents.

Worth the Journey: The Train Ride to Glory

There is more to the story, but reading the **actual** book is more fulfilling. Points that may be drawn from this brief summary are:

1. We may not be able to take loved-ones on our spiritual journey.
2. God will supply help from unexpected sources along the way.
3. You are given weapons to combat the devil.
4. Temptations will try to hinder your progress.
5. The closer you get to the goal, the stronger opposition will be.
6. There is a river to cross referred to as the "River of Life" in the Book of Revelation.
7. When you reach Heaven, you **WILL BE WELCOMED!**

Marlowe R. Scott

Questions for Consideration

1. What mountains and hindrances have you experienced in your journey?

Worth the Journey: The Train Ride to Glory

2. How did you overcome them?

3. Did you question the "why" of your problems when you felt you didn't deserve them?

Worth the Journey: The Train Ride to Glory

4. As you have grown in your spiritual walk, does looking back let you know you are stronger?

_____

_____

_____

_____

_____

_____

_____

_____

_____

_____

_____

_____

CHAPTER FOUR
HIGH PLACES

Worth the Journey: The Train Ride to Glory

When thinking about the song *Lift Him Up* that was shared earlier, my thoughts went to those scriptures about hind's feet in high places, because the Cross of Jesus was erected on Calvary – a high place for ALL to see.

The following scriptures speak of having our feet set on high places - mountains for example - like a hind. Again, my desire to learn more lead to researching what a "hind" is and I discovered an astonishing fact: The hind is a female deer of the red deer species. The male of the species is called a hart. As with many of God's creation, the hind's size varies due to the geographical location in which she lives. She generally weighs between 120 to 170 pounds.

Marlowe R. Scott

2 Samuel 22:32-37

32. For who is God, save the LORD?
and who is a rock, save our God?
33. God is my strength and power:
and he maketh my way perfect.
34. He maketh my feet like hinds' feet:
and setteth me upon my high places.
35. He teacheth my hands to war; so that a
bow of steel is broken by mine arms.
36. Thou hast also given me the shield of thy
salvation:
and thy gentleness hath made me great.
37. Thou hast enlarged my steps under me;
so that my feet did not slip.

Worth the Journey: The Train Ride to Glory

Psalms 18:31-35

31. For who is God save the LORD?

Or who is a rock save our God?

32. It is God that girdeth me with strength,

and maketh my way perfect.

33. He maketh my feet like hinds feet,

and setteth me upon my high places.

34. He teacheth my hands to war, so that a

bow of steel is broken by mine arms.

35. Thou hast also given me the shield of thy

salvation:

and thy right hand holden me up,

and thy gentleness hath made me great.

Marlowe R. Scott

Habakkak 3:17-19

17. Although the fig tree shall not blossom, neither shall fruit be in the vines; the labour of the olive shall fail, and the fields shall yield no meat; the flock shall be cut off from the fold,
and there shall be no herd in the stalls:
18. Yet I will rejoice in the LORD,
I will joy in the God of my salvation.
19. The LORD God is my strength, and he will make my feet like hinds' feet, and he will make me walk upon mine high places. To the chief singer on my stringed instruments.

Worth the Journey: The Train Ride to Glory

These scriptures give important spiritual lessons on being like a hind:

- Our feet will not slip – go backward down the mountains we have climbed.
- With strength and perfection, we are blessed to set in high places and taught to fight spiritual battles with proper armor and support.
- We are to rejoice in the Lord - no matter what is going on around us - and continue walking in those high places.

Marlowe R. Scott

Questions for Consideration

1. In addition to the three scriptural passages stated, how does the hind relate to your Christian journey?

Worth the Journey: The Train Ride to Glory

2. Scripture often uses God's creation to teach valuable lessons. Take a few minutes to jot down other animals or vegetation used to teach us.

3. Both the Old (2 Samuel 22:36 and Psalm 18:35) and New Testaments (Ephesians 6:13-17) speak of spiritual armor. When have you used spiritual armor to overcome the wiles of the devil?

CHAPTER FIVE
PRESSING UPWARD

Marlowe R. Scott

Much like the Epistle of Paul in Philippians 3:14, Christians are to "press" to the mark of the prize of the high calling of God in Jesus Christ. Another great hymn by Johnson Oatman, Jr. is fitting to note: *Higher Ground* (also known as *I'm Pressing on the Upward Way*).

Worth the Journey: The Train Ride to Glory

HIGHER GROUND

I'm pressing on the upward way,
New heights I'm gaining every day;
Still praying as I'm onward bound,
"Lord, plant my feet on higher ground."

Refrain:
Lord, lift me up and let me stand,
By faith, on Heaven's tableland,:
A higher plane that I have found;
Lord, plant my feet on higher ground.

My heart has no desire to stay
Where doubts arise and fears dismay;
Though some may dwell where those abound,
My prayer, my aim, is higher ground.

I want to live above the world,
Though Satan's darts at me are hurled;
For faith has caught the joyful sound,
The song of saints on higher ground.

I want to scale the upmost height
And catch a gleam of glory bright;
But still I'll pray till heav'n I've found,
"Lord, plant my feet on higher ground."

Marlowe R. Scott

CALVARY'S CROSS – A POEM

Jesus Christ gives us eternal life through His bearing of our sins on the Cross of Calvary in a place also called Golgotha (The Place of the Skull). The following poem, *Calvary's Cross*, shares my attempt to convey a message to point others to Our Savior Jesus Christ.

Worth the Journey: The Train Ride to Glory

CALVARY'S CROSS
Marlowe R. Scott © 2016

The song writer wrote there's a cross for everyone
Yes, crosses for you and me
The crosses we bear may be many
But each has a message and lesson you see.

There is a cross that is more precious than them all
It is The Cross on Calvary
That rugged Cross that Our Savior bore
To save sinners like you and me.

Jesus was crucified on that cross
On the hill named Calvary.
As between two sinners the cross stood
As He bore the sins for you and me.

He died and was placed in a borrowed tomb
Where His body stayed until early on the third day
Then, He rose with all authority in Heaven and earth
On that very first Easter Day!

After 40 days before His ascension to Glory
Jesus promised the Holy Spirit's power would come
So that mankind would become witnesses in all the Earth
Because of Salvation given by God's One and Only Son.

Now, we must seek forgiveness and tell the world
That the free gift of Salvation is here
To anyone admitting sin and believing in Jesus
The One who sacrificed His life because He loved us so dear.

Questions for Consideration

1. How have songs and/or poetry blessed and comforted you spiritually?

Worth the Journey: The Train Ride to Glory

2.   What are some of your favorites? Why not take time to share them with family and friends?

_____

_____

_____

_____

_____

_____

_____

_____

_____

_____

_____

_____

CHAPTER SIX
THE EMPTY CROSS

Worth the Journey: The Train Ride to Glory

The Crucifix and the Cross

As the empty Cross symbolizes so much to our Christian journey, the following is meant to share my deepest personal beliefs and understanding of that symbol.

Jewelry designers, sculptors, and clothing manufacturers have (over the years) shown Jesus Christ, our **RISEN** Savior, nailed on a cross. The information that follows is not meant to criticize or change anyone's religion or beliefs; however, it is meant to share an important *fact* which some may not have thought about.

Christians believe that our Savior, Jesus Christ, was taken off Calvary's Cross, laid in a tomb, and on the third day after his crucifixion, rose again. For Jesus to be displayed on a cross with a crown of thorns is not scripturally correct. **HE IS NOT ON A CROSS ANYMORE!** That is why we celebrate Easter (or Resurrection Day)!

The scripture quote written by Paul from Colossians 3:1 makes it quite clear where Jesus is: "If ye then be risen with Christ, seek those things which are above, *where Christ sitteth on the right hand of God*" (emphasis added).

Marlowe R. Scott

Questions for Consideration

1. Have you ever thought about the empty cross and Jesus not being there and suffering anymore? Explain your thoughts.

_____

_____

_____

_____

_____

_____

_____

_____

_____

_____

_____

_____

Worth the Journey: The Train Ride to Glory

2. Is your belief that Colossians 3:1 is incorrect? Should you have a different belief? Explain.

CONCLUSION

It is imperative that we be "real" in our worship to God and His Precious Son, Jesus Christ. This includes interactions with our brothers and sisters who are not only within the body of Christ, but also those who are without the ark of safety found through salvation. As an old saying goes, "Sometimes, the only sermon a person may see is you!" We never know who may be turned away from or drawn into Christianity by our actions and words.

While each journey is unique, the goal is the same. We are to be witnesses while here on Earth and draw others to Jesus Christ. Plant seeds of love and have compassion as you and I point others to Heaven!

Worth the Journey: The Train Ride to Glory

BENEDICTION

Colossians 3:16-17

*"Let the word of Christ dwell in you richly in all wisdom; teaching and admonishing one another in psalms and hymns and spiritual songs, singing with grace in your hearts to the LORD.
And whatsoever ye do in word or deed, do all in the name of the Lord Jesus, giving thanks to God and the Father by him."*
Amen.

Worth the Journey - Conclusion

Prayerfully, the unchanging messages of the gospel have made a difference in your life as well as those you encounter on life's journey. The message of the Holy Scriptures has not changed in this fast-paced world we live in:

- Jesus Christ is the promised Messiah prophesized in the Old Testament.
- Jesus is part of the Holy Trinity: Father, Son, and Holy Spirit.
- He came in human form to teach mankind and to show His love and compassion while pointing to a Heavenly reward for those who accept Him.
- He willingly sacrificed His life for all who would repent and believe in Him.
- Heaven is a REAL place for the repentant souls of saved believers in Jesus Christ.

Amen.

~ Author Marlowe R. Scott ~

TESTIMONIES and INSIGHTS

Written reviews and comments are provided from some who have shared inspirations and strength received from reading my two previous books *Spiritual Growth: From Milk to Strong Meat* and *Believing Without Seeing: The Power of Faith.*

Rev. Margaret Jackson, Pulpit Staff, Tabernacle Baptist Church
"Marlowe: Thank you for sharing your heart. Your publication, Spiritual Growth: From Milk to Strong meat, is encouraging and inspirational. I applaud you for your willingness to stand up for the Kingdom of God, sharing your poetry and life experiences."

Claretha Mervin, Educator and Youth Mentor
"I enjoyed reading Spiritual Growth from Milk to Strong Meat and I would recommend it to any of my friends. This book was an encouragement to me letting me know every day is not going to be easy, but I can grow as I go through the storms of life."

Cousin Marian Wynder, Missionary President, AME Church Member
"Spiritual Growth: From Milk to Strong Meat was very good reading for all ages. The journey the book took us on was informative, insightful and relatable. I shared the book with a friend who also enjoy it and was inspired."

Beverly Jackson, CMSgt (Ret)
"I loved Spiritual Growth: From Milk to Strong Meat. I know Marlowe Scott personally and she walks the life she wrote about. A lot of her experiences are shared in the book I found relates to my life also. She just poetically put it in a very interesting format to bring humor to her life experience in lieu of sadness. I have read it again and again on down days to bring me back to reality and remind me how blessed I really am. I purchased several copies and gave as gifts to my church family members."

Worth the Journey: The Train Ride to Glory

Mary Lanterman, Retired Banker and Prolific Quilter
"Inspirational and encouraging reading for sure. With God guiding my life and friends like you to light the path, serenity can only be ahead!"

Elder Valerie Pernell, St. John Pentecostal Church
"My aunt lent me your book. It's absolutely beautiful. It didn't feel like I was reading a book. It felt like I was having a beautiful conversation with the author, YOU. Life's Railroad to Heaven was a song my mother loved and I love it myself, in fact I need to sing this again...it's been a very long time since I sang this song. Please continue to do whatever the Lord instructs you to do."

Jennifer Mervin, Educator
"Your book was an inspiration to me. Some days I become very weary of my faith and began to doubt what God has planned for my life, but when I look back over my life and see what God has brought you through, it allows for me to resume my faith in him because he blessed me with so much and has brought me a mighty long way."

Marlowe R. Scott

CMSgt Henry C. Whitman, Jr., Retired USAF
"Growing up in the Methodist Church and having a special needs relative, I was amazed how indistinguishable many of our life experiences were. Reading your first book, Spiritual Growth: From Milk to Strong Meat was like "COMING HOME".

Harry Addison, Jr, Retired Engineer and Church Trustee
"Believing Without Seeing is an inspiring book. Marlowe Scott explains how to use Bible study and our God-given gifts to obtain peace of mind and live a Christian life."

Sally Hatcher, Educator
"Both books were very inspiring to me. There were small spoken words that meant so much to me. The books filled my soul and spirit. They depicted life's layout and the struggles we face day by day. The hard and difficulties on life's journey were captivated. Finally, it was clear on how we as a people should live – love and have faith as ordained by God."

Elder and Cousin Arlene Holden, Bethel Pentecostal Church
"Your books are blessings to those who read them because you wrote them from your life experiences. Through reading your story, others may choose to trust God and approach their everyday lives with positive attitudes."

Amazon Best-Selling Books Written by Marlowe R. Scott

Spiritual Growth: From Milk to Strong Meat
2015 Pearly Gates Publishing, LLC
Angela Edwards, CEO

AMAZON BEST-SELLER
Available for purchase at:
http://bit.ly/MilkToMeat

Marlowe R. Scott

Believing Without Seeing: The Power of Faith
2015 Pearly Gates Publishing, LLC
Angela Edwards, CEO

AMAZON BEST-SELLER
Available for purchase at:
http://bit.ly/BelievingWithoutSeeing

Worth the Journey: The Train Ride to Glory

Keeping It Real: The Straight and Narrow
2016 Pearly Gates Publishing, LLC
Angela Edwards, CEO

AMAZON BEST-SELLER
Available for purchase at:
http://bit.ly/KIRPbk

ABOUT THE AUTHOR

Marlowe R. Scott was born at home in a small, South Jersey community of Cedarville, New Jersey. Her parents were Carl and Helena Harris. Marlowe is a true country girl who loves nature – God's wondrous creation. She enjoys seeing birds preparing nests, wild turkeys roaming the backyard with their young, and the stately deer in the field and property tree line where she lives in Browns Mills, New Jersey.

Worth the Journey: The Train Ride to Glory

Marlowe has been blessed with many talents. They include: writing, poetry, music, sewing, crocheting, quilting, and floral designs. Her educational focus was the Communications Arts Degree Program at Burlington County College, as well as attendance and participation in numerous government-sponsored training venues. Marlowe's extensive experiences encompassed duties as: Leadership, Education, and Development Facilitator; Equal Employment Opportunity Counselor; Quality Management Facilitator; and member of the New Jersey Quality Board of Examiners. With her commitment to quality, she also participated in videoconferences, workshops, and community volunteer activities. One highlight of her career was a conference held in Baltimore, Maryland where she was a member of a select group of individuals who met and interacted with Retired U.S. Army General and Former U.S. Secretary of State, Colin Powell. Marlowe retired after 33 years of dedicated federal civil service.

Marlowe R. Scott

She has taught Floral Arts and Crafts in adult education, won ribbons for her creative designs, and appeared on television. Currently, she devotes most of her time to quilting and developing her home-based business, *M.R.S. Inspirations*, with the motto "Magnificent Revelations are My Specialty". Her creations are focused on making special memories in lap quilts, throws, baby quilts, and pillows which show love and give comfort to the recipient.

Marlowe is married to Andrew Scott and has three children: Carl, James, and Angela, as well as five grandchildren and eight great-grandchildren. She is currently a member of Tabernacle Baptist Church, Burlington, New Jersey.

Worth the Journey: The Train Ride to Glory

M.R.S. Inspirations
Magnificent Revelations Are My Speciality

Marlowe R. Scott
Owner/Creator

Phone: (609) 248-0051
Email: M.R.BOYCE4491@gmail.com
Browns Mills, NJ

"Specializing in Hand-Crafted Creations Giving Special Comfort and LOVE"

- ➢ Memory Pillows
- ➢ Memory Quilts
- ➢ Crib Quilts
- ➢ Throws
- ➢ And much, much more!